D1555795

BrightRED Revision

Higher
BUSINESS
MANAGEMENT

Moira Stephen and
Caroline Patterson

BrightRED
PUBLISHING

First published in 2010 by:
Bright Red Publishing Ltd
6 Stafford Street
Edinburgh
EH3 7AU

Copyright © Bright Red Publishing Ltd 2010

Cover image © Caleb Rutherford

All rights reserved. No part of this publication may be reproduced, stored in a retrieval system, or transmitted in any form or by any means, electronic, mechanical, photocopying, recording or otherwise, without prior permission in writing from the publisher.

The rights of Caroline Patterson and Moira Stephen to be identified as the authors of this work has been asserted by them in accordance with sections 77 and 78 of the Copyright, Designs and Patents Act 1988

A CIP record for this book is available from the British Library

ISBN 978-1-906736-18-7

With thanks to:
The Partnership Publishing Solutions (layout) and Alex Hepworth (copy-edit)

Cover design by Caleb Rutherford – e i d e t i c

Illustrations by Artlife Designs

Every effort has been made to seek all copyright-holders. If any have been overlooked, then Bright Red Publishing will be delighted to make the necessary arrangements.

Bright Red Publishing is grateful for the use of the following:
Logo © British Heart Foundation (page 10); Logo © the National Trust for Scotland (page 10); Logo © The Duke of Edinburgh's Award (page 10); Logo © BBC (page 11); Logo © Royal Mail (page 11); Logo © Fake Bake (page 12); Article from The Scotsman, 29 August 2009 © Johnston Press Plc (page 13); Logo © The Body Shop (page 13); Logo © SUBWAY® Restaurants (page 13); Logo © Perfect Pizza Ltd (page 13); Logo © The Prince's Scottish Youth Business Trust (page 18); Photo © Shaun Egan/The Image Bank/Getty Images (page 26); Photo © Andi Collington (page 26); An article from BBC News, 31 March 2009, http://news.bbc.co.uk/1/hi/england/lancashire/7974830.stm (page 29); Photo © Andi Collington (page 30); Photo © Andi Collington (page 30); Photo © Andi Collington (page 32); Photo © Chris Jackson/Getty Images Entertainment/Getty Images (page 49); Photo © EasyJet (page 49); Article from Business Scotsman, 11 April 2009 © Johnston Press Plc (page 51); Photo © Macsween of Edinburgh (page 51); Data provided by Net Market Share http://www.netmarketshare.com/search-engine-market-share.aspx?qprid=4 (page 52); Article from Edinburgh Evening News, 23 May 2009 © Johnston Press Plc (page 53); The Kitemark © BSI (www.Kitemark.com) (page 69); The Red Lion logo © Britegg (page 69); Article from Edinburgh Evening News, 16 September 2009 © Johnston Press Plc (page 77); Photo © TORSTEN BLACKWOOD/AFP/Getty Images (page 79); Article from The Scotsman, 11 May 2009 © Johnston Press Plc (page 81); Photo © Serge Krouglikoff/Stone/Getty Images (page 82); An article from BBC News 18 May 2009 http://news.bbc.co.uk/1/hi/england/wiltshire/8056098.stm (page 85); Cartoon © Carroll Zahn, www.cartoonstock.com (page 89); Article from The Scotsman, 19 June 2009 © Johnston Press Plc (page 91); An extract from 'MPs to have spotlight on expenses' by Paul Waugh. Originally published in: Evening Standard 15/06/2007 © Evening Standard (page 93).

Printed and bound in Scotland by Scotprint

Mixed Sources
Product group from well-managed forests and other controlled sources
www.fsc.org Cert no. TT-COC-002217
FSC © 1996 Forest Stewardship Council

CONTENTS

1 INTRODUCTION

COURSE STRUCTURE

The Higher Business Management course is divided into three units:

- Unit 1 Business Enterprise
- Unit 2 Business Decision Areas: Marketing and Operations
- Unit 3 Business Decision Areas: Finance and Human Resource Management

ASSESSMENT

The Higher Business Management course is assessed in the following ways:

NABs

Each of the three units is assessed within your school/college using a National Assessment Bank test. NABs are set by the Scottish Qualifications Authority, and the assessment for each unit consists of a closed-book assessment which should take a maximum of 60 minutes. The cut-off score for the NABs is 20 marks out of 40, meaning that you need 50 per cent to pass.

The exam

You will also take an externally-assessed written examination which will last 2.5 hours and has 100 marks available. The paper consists of two sections.

Section 1 (total marks for this section: 50)

Section 1 consists of a case study of about 750 words which focuses on a situation facing an organisation or business. It will be based on a real situation. You will be asked to answer a set number of questions from this case study. The first question (worth 10 marks) usually asks you to identify the problems that exist in the case study under the following headings:

1 Marketing

2 Finance

3 Operations

4 Human resources

5 External factors.

The remaining questions expect you to be able to:

- analyse the information given
- identify and assess constraints
- devise solutions and make recommendations
- justify your recommendations.

Remember that half-marks are **not** awarded, so you must make sure not to give one-word answers – always **develop** your point.

Section 2 (total marks for this section: 50)

This part of the paper assesses knowledge and understanding. It consists of five questions taken from any part of the course. You must answer only **two questions.** You need to be able to write extended answers – and each question is worth 25 marks.

DON'T FORGET

You can access the Scottish Qualifications Authority's website at **www.sqa. org.uk**. If you select NQ, then the subject Business Management, you can follow the links to the Principal Assessor Report, Past Papers and Marking Schemes.

THE STRUCTURE AND AIM OF THIS BOOK

The aim of this book is to present the content of the course for Higher Business Management in an easy-to-read and understandable format. It does not go into the detail of a full textbook, and it is recommended that you use it along with notes provided by your teacher or with other textbooks.

The book is divided into three chapters – one for each unit. The section on **internal organisation** (see pages 42–49) is not assessed in the internal units (NABs). Topics are presented in double-page spreads which:

- provide key ideas and concepts for the topic being studied
- contain internet links and 'Don't forget' boxes to draw your attention to important pieces of knowledge or further reading
- contain a 'Let's think about this' reflection point. Sometimes this is a case study, sometimes a question and sometimes an internet link to further information or study.

The table below summarises the key terms or 'command words' used in the exam questions. If you write in bullet points, you must give examples and develop your points in accordance with the command word and the number of marks allocated to that question. In general, 'Explain' is the command word that causes candidates the most difficulty.

Command word	What does it mean?
Compare	Give the differences and similarities between the two options – try to use words and phrases such as **whereas** or **on the other hand** in your answer.
Describe	Give a definition and then an example or explanation of what you mean.
Discuss	Consider different points in your answer, perhaps by giving advantages and disadvantages. Offer reasons for and against what you are saying.
Distinguish	Identify the differences between two or more items.
Explain	Give a detailed response. You will need to provide a definition, followed by explanation and examples.
Identify	Name or categorise items.
Justify	Give reasons – make sure you answer **why** something is needed. Support your answer with suggestions or conclusions.
Outline	This is basically a description without too much detail.

DON'T FORGET

Learning and Teaching Scotland have some resources that you may find useful. Access their website at www.ltscotland. org.uk/nq/subjects/ businessmanagement. asp

THE ROLE OF BUSINESS IN CONTEMPORARY SOCIETY

Today's society has many needs and wants – for essential goods and services (food, clothes, hospitals, schools or transport) as well as for discretionary items and services (things we like to have, but could do without).

Business activity describes any activity that provides us with the goods and services to satisfy our wants. The **output** of business activity is the goods and services we require or desire.

THE BUSINESS CYCLE

Business activity can be illustrated using the **business cycle**.

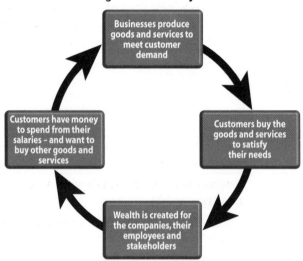

DON'T FORGET

A **market** is where buying and selling takes place; for example, on the internet, in the town centre, on the stock exchange or at a trade fair.

The more business activity there is, and the more goods and services a country produces, the **wealthier** it is. So, the more we produce, the wealthier we become.

PRODUCTION AND CONSUMPTION OF GOODS AND SERVICES

Goods can be classified as:

- **durable** – they can be used several times and are long-lasting; for example, cars, washing machines and computers

or

- **non-durable** – they are normally used only once or are perishable; for example, food, drink and newspapers.

There are **four factors of production**:

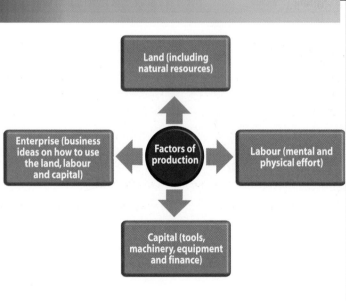

DON'T FORGET

CELL = Capital, Enterprise, Land and Labour.

SECTORS OF ACTIVITY

There are **three sectors of business activity**.

Primary sector

- Businesses involved in exploiting and extracting natural resources.
- In the UK, this sector has declined over the past 40 years.
- Examples include farming, mining, forestry, drilling for oil and trawling for fish.

Secondary sector

- Businesses involved in manufacturing and construction (businesses that make and build things).
- In the UK, this sector has also declined over the past 40 years.
- Examples include car manufacture, construction, shipbuilding and the building of roads and bridges.

Tertiary sector

- Businesses providing a commercial service.
- In the UK, this sector has been growing at the expense of the primary and secondary sectors.
- Examples include banking, tourism, shops, hotels, education, insurance and health care.

For an explanation of why secondary-sector industries have declined in the UK, read the article at: www.trial.eunits.co.uk/html/secondary_sector.html

LET'S THINK ABOUT THIS

Read this quote taken from the website below. Can you give examples of industries that have been particularly affected by this in the UK? For each example you give, find out where the competition came from. What effect did it have on the local community?

'Manufacturing tends to be more open to international trade and competition than services. As a result, there has been a tendency for the first economies to industrialize to come under competitive attack by those seeking to industrialize later, e.g. because production, especially labour, costs are lower in those industrializing later.'

www.businesspme.com/uk/articles/production/37/The-tertiary-sector-of-industry.html

PRIVATE-SECTOR ORGANISATIONS

SOLE TRADER

This type of business has ONE owner. It is very easy to set up, but work may have to stop if the owner is ill or on holiday.

Advantages	Disadvantages
Owner gets all the profits.	Owner has unlimited liability.
Owner has control over decisions.	Owner has limited access to finance.
Owner can choose own hours and holidays.	Owner has no-one to share problems/decisions with.
Owner can give personal service to customers.	Owner has no-one to share workload.

PARTNERSHIP

This type of business can have 2–20 partners and must have a Partnership Agreement.

Advantages	Disadvantages
Wider range of expertise than sole trader.	Unlimited liability.
More financing options.	Profits shared between more people.
Shared workload.	Possible disagreements.
Easier to raise finance from lenders than for a sole trader.	New Partnership Agreement needed if someone leaves or dies.

PRIVATE LIMITED COMPANY (LTD)

This is a company with privately-owned shares (it is not on the stock market). It is usually a family business and must have a minimum of one shareholder and be run by a director or board of directors. It must produce a Memorandum of Association and Articles of Association.

Advantages	Disadvantages
Shareholders have limited liability.	Profits shared between more people.
Control of company not lost to outsiders.	There is a legal process in setting up the company.
More finance can be raised from shareholders and lenders.	Shares cannot be sold to the public.
Significant experience and expertise from shareholders and directors.	Firm has to abide by requirements of the Companies Act.
	Annual accounts must be presented to Companies House in Edinburgh (for Scottish-based firms).

PUBLIC LIMITED COMPANY (PLC)

This type of company sells its shares on the stock market – the company is owned by the shareholders. It must have a minimum of two shareholders and £50 000 share capital. It must produce a Memorandum of Association and Articles of Association.

Advantages	Disadvantages
Can raise large amounts of finance.	Set-up costs can be high.
Plcs often dominate their markets.	Must abide by Companies Act.
Comparatively easy to borrow money from lenders.	No control over who buys shares.
Shareholders have limited liability.	Must publish annual accounts.

The following link will give you a useful summary of the differences between a private limited company and a public limited company: www.businesslink.gov.uk/bdotg/action/detail?type=RESOURCES&itemId=1073789599

DON'T FORGET

A **multinational** is a large plc that has manufacturing plants in more than one country; for example, Shell. These very large organisations can benefit from economies of scale, avoidance of import restrictions or home-country legislation that might restrict their activities, and tax advantages and grants from other governments.

SOURCES OF FINANCE FOR DIFFERENT TYPES OF BUSINESS

	Own money	Retained profits	Bank loan	Bank overdraft	Government grants	Trade credit	Debt factoring	New partner	New shareholder	Selling shares to public	Issue debentures
Sole trader	✓	✓	✓	✓	✓	✓	✓				
Partnership	✓	✓	✓	✓	✓	✓	✓	✓			
Ltd		✓	✓	✓	✓	✓	✓		✓		
Plc		✓	✓	✓	✓	✓	✓			✓	✓

Other methods of raising finance could include a commercial mortgage, selling assets or land, venture capitalists and using retained profits.

COMPANY OBJECTIVES IN RAISING FINANCE

	Survival	Maximise profits	Improve personal status	Good community image	Growth	Strong status	Highest possible sales revenue	Expand output	Increase sales revenue	Dominate market	Strong image
Sole trader	✓	✓	✓	✓	✓		✓	✓			
Partnership	✓	✓	✓	✓	✓		✓	✓			
Ltd	✓	✓		✓	✓	✓	✓	✓			
Plc	✓	✓		✓	✓	✓	✓	✓	✓	✓	✓

DON'T FORGET

Unlimited liability means that, if the company fails, the owner or investor can lose any **personal** assets; for example, their house, savings or car.

 **LET'S THINK ABOUT THIS**

Lastminute.com is a private company that went public on 14 March 2000. Follow the link below and read the article. What does 'going public' mean? The term IPO is often used when discussing flotation. What does IPO stand for? Do you think there would be the same frenzy for shares in Lastminute.com in today's economic climate? Why?
http://news.bbc.co.uk/1/hi/business/671434.stm

OTHER TYPES OF ORGANISATIONS

NON-PROFIT-MAKING ORGANISATIONS

Non-profit-making organisations can be either charities or voluntary organisations.

Charities

- regulated by the government – Register of Charities
- exempt from paying some taxes
- often set up as trusts with no individual owner
- overall control and management by a board of trustees
- trustees unpaid
- volunteers do a lot of the day-to-day fundraising
- finance
  - donations
  - government grants
  - profits from their own shops
  - sale of goods
  - raffles
  - jumble sales
- objectives
  - provide a service
  - relieve poverty
  - fund research

Voluntary organisations

- staffed by volunteers
- run by a committee of elected members
- finance
  - grants from the National Lottery, Sports Council or local authority
  - membership fees
  - charge for facilities
- objectives
  - bring people with similar interests together (for example, a local residents' association or Scouting group)

the National Trust
for Scotland
a place for everyone

DON'T FORGET

Charities and voluntary organisations are non-profit-making. Any surplus they make is used to support the objectives of the organisation.

There are a huge number of charities and voluntary organisations in the UK. You could check out the following links to see the main aims and objectives of a few.
www.nts.org.uk/About/
www.barnardos.org.uk/scotland.htm
www.DofE.org/en/content/cms/About_Us/About_Us.aspx
www.bhf.org.uk/

PUBLICLY-FUNDED ORGANISATIONS

These organisations are owned by the taxpayer and controlled by local or central government. They provide a service for everyone and tend to face little competition. The service they provide, although often essential, may be unprofitable if provided by private businesses.

Local government

- set up by central government
- run by locally-elected councillors
- day-to-day running by managers and employees
- provide a range of services (for example, education, refuse collection or housing)
- objectives: meet local needs, provide a wide range of services, make cost savings, adhere to agreed budgets
- finance: comes from central government

Central government

- government in Westminster and the Scottish Parliament
- provide national services (for example, defence, health and transport, treasury, trade and industry)
- policies and direction come from elected politicians
- departments run by employed civil servants
- objectives: provide a service, improve society, make effective use of funds and taxes
- finance: comes from taxes

Public corporations

- owned by central government
- government minister appoints a chairperson and board of directors
- objectives: provide quality service, make best use of funds, serve public interests, perform better than rivals
- finance: grants from government, money raised from the public (for example, by selling merchandise or licence fees)
- examples include the BBC, Scottish Water, Highlands & Islands Airports

 **DON'T FORGET**

Publicly-funded organisations such as the police service, the National Health Service and Learning and Teaching Scotland are non-profit-making organisations that are owned by the taxpayer and controlled by the government. Public limited companies are private-sector organisations whose main objectives include maximising profits, increasing sales, dominating the market and growth.

 This link will help you to understand publicly-funded organisations:
www.bbc.co.uk/schools/gcsebitesize/business/aims/publicsectorrev1.shtml

LET'S THINK ABOUT THIS

Edinburgh Community Backgreens Association is an example of a voluntary organisation, while **Friends of Loch Lomond and the Trossachs** is a registered charity. Look at their websites and identify the main differences between them.
www.ecba.org.uk/home.aspx
www.lochlomondtrossachs.org.uk/

ENTREPRENEURSHIP AND FRANCHISING

ENTREPRENEURS

An entrepreneur has many skills, from spotting a business opportunity to working through all the stages required to make it a success. Within an organisation, an entrepreneur will delegate responsibility to managers or staff once he or she has got an idea off the ground.

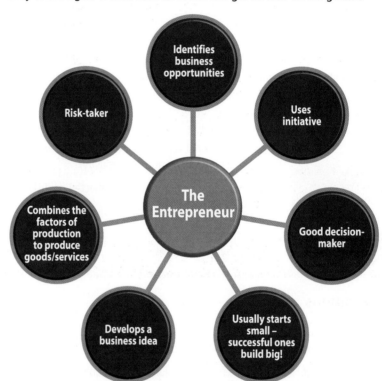

DON'T FORGET

In an entrepreneurial structure, there are only one or two key decision-makers.

The Deli on the Corner in Stewarton, Ayrshire started trading in 2006. Concentrating on quality local produce, it has since extended its activities to include catering for events, hampers and an online shop which has opened up a wider market. Its achievements were recognised when it was made **Scottish regional winner Most Promising New Business 2008** by the British Chamber of Commerce and Industry.

 www.delionthecorner.co.uk/

Fake Bake is another high-profile example of recent successful entrepreneurial activity. Having started her beauty salon selling the products of an American company, Fake Bake owner Sandra McClumpha went on to buy out the parent company in 2008.

In 2006, Sandra was awarded the **NatWest Everywoman Award** – and, in 2007, the *Sunday Times* congratulated her on her achievements.

DON'T FORGET

An entrepreneur has to be able to identify strategic and tactical objectives for a business idea.

 www.fakebake.co.uk/sandra-mcclumpha.php

You will find lots of examples of entrepreneurs pitching for financial aid in the television programme *Dragons' Den*.
www.bbc.co.uk/dragonsden/

FRANCHISING

Many of the UK's best-known businesses are franchises.

- Subway has over 31 000 franchises in 90 countries.
- The Body Shop has over 2500 shops in over 60 countries.
- Perfect Pizza has more than 110 stores across the UK.
- Apollo Blinds has 85 retail outlets in the UK and Ireland.
- Burger King has more than 11 000 restaurants in over 60 countries.

A **franchise** is a **business agreement** between a **franchiser** (the business whose name is used, for example Perfect Pizza) and a **franchisee** (the person or people who want to set up a business). A franchisee can set up any type of business.

The franchisee benefits from having an established image and brand to sell. The franchiser will often provide training and help to furnish the business. They will also be able to provide advice and guidance to the franchisee if required.

A potential disadvantage for the franchisee is that they are not free to develop their business as they wish – the products they sell, and the image they have, will be determined by the franchiser.

The franchiser benefits, as they can increase their market share without investing further capital; the franchiser is paid a percentage of profits or sales – or a royalty – and can control the way the business is run.

DON'T FORGET

You should be aware of the advantages and disadvantages of a franchise agreement – from the point of view of both the **franchiser** and the **franchisee**.

You will find a brief, but useful, summary of franchising at:
www.thebfa.org/whatis.asp

LET'S THINK ABOUT THIS

Read this article. In the current economic climate, what characteristics do you think will be identified as those of the successful (or potentially successful) entrepreneur?

Will we see entrepreneurs' softer side as reality bites in recession?

Entrepreneurship, it would appear, is everywhere these days. Thank *Dragons' Den* and *The Apprentice* for catchphrases such as 'I'm out!' and 'You're fired'.

Not that all self-made business types are hard-nosed mavericks like Duncan Bannatyne and Sir Alan Sugar – a point that academics are hoping to highlight as they embark on new research.

Dr Rob Smith, a lecturer at Aberdeen's Robert Gordon University, is looking to change the way we think about entrepreneurs, in light of the current economic crisis.

Smith, who is co-editing a special edition of a prestigious international journal, is inviting contributions that consider how alternative accounts of entrepreneurship 'may shape or be shaped by a changing economic order'.

Scotsman, 29 August 2009

BUSINESS OBJECTIVES

All organisations have objectives, or goals. Having a clear understanding of an organisation's objectives is crucial when it comes to decision-making. Objectives give a clearly-defined target for the organisation and provide the focus for planning and decision-making.

Typical corporate objectives include:

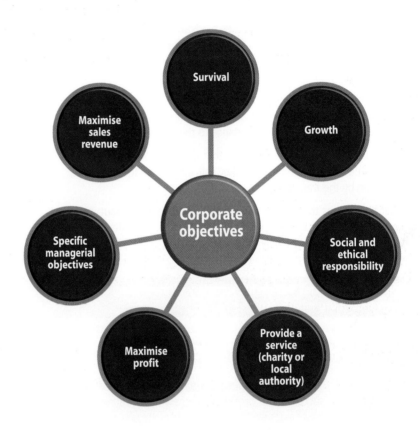

SMART

Remember that business objectives should be **SMART**:

S	Specific	Objectives are specific to what the business does. For example, a hospital might have the objective of decreasing waiting lists for non-urgent operations by 15 per cent within the next calendar year.
M	Measurable	The business must be able to measure progress; for example, the income from sales in the next six months.
A	Agreed	All those concerned must be in agreement about the objective.
R	Realistic	The objective should be challenging, but also achievable given the resources available.
T	Time-specific	There should be an agreed time scale for achieving the objective.

DON'T FORGET

You must be able to relate different objectives to different types of organisation.

Look up http://tutor2u.net/economics/gcse/revision_notes/firms_objectives.htm

TYPES OF OBJECTIVES

Different types of companies will have different objectives. Depending on the ambitions and beliefs of the managers, a company may not even have the objective of maximising profit.

Objectives depend on:	Objectives may not be achieved because of:	Other organisational aims:
size of organisation	competition	protect the environment
age of company	environment	promote equal opportunity
state of company	law	eliminate discrimination
whether in the public or private sector	political situation	
company policy	shareholder demands	
company's financial situation	owners	
use of technology	society	
	industrial relations (for example, disputes with staff)	

DON'T FORGET

Both **internal** and **external** factors can influence whether or not a company is successful in achieving its objectives.

 A key objective for many organisations in a recession is survival. Read how British Airways is proposing to meet this objective at: http://news.bbc.co.uk/1/hi/business/8149082.stm

LET'S THINK ABOUT THIS

Tunnock's (manufacturers of the Caramel Wafer®) is a **private limited company**. Cadbury is a **public limited company** recently bought over by Kraft Foods. Visit the websites of these two companies to find out a bit about both.

www.tunnock.co.uk/

www.cadbury.co.uk/home/Pages/home.aspx

DON'T FORGET

Managers are responsible for organisations meeting their objectives and must plan, organise, command, coordinate and control. This means they must have experience and understanding, as well as excellent interpersonal and decision-making skills.

STAKEHOLDERS

A stakeholder is any person, organisation or group that has an interest in the **success** of an organisation. Stakeholders can be internal or external, and different types of organisation will have different stakeholders.

Being able to name stakeholders is not enough – you must be able to discuss their **interest** in the organisation and also what **influence** they can have on organisational objectives and behaviour.

INTERNAL STAKEHOLDERS

Stakeholder	Interest	Influence
Employees	Salary Job satisfaction Working conditions Job security	Standard of work Industrial relations (for example, strike action)
Managers	Salary Bonuses Responsibility Status	Hiring staff Product portfolio Industrial relations (for example, can antagonise workers)
Shareholders	Want company to be successful Dividends Improved share value	Vote for directors Approve dividend payments Can protest against decisions (for example, large salary increases) Can sell shares (may affect company image if done on large scale)

DON'T FORGET

Discuss **appropriate** stakeholders depending on the question. For example, an **investor** would not be an appropriate stakeholder in a question asking about stakeholders in a local council.

DON'T FORGET

There is a difference between a stakeholder's **interest** in an organisation and their **influence** on it.

 Successful companies take their stakeholders very seriously. Many publish details of how they are (or how they propose) to get feedback from their stakeholders. You can read about how Virgin Media talk to their stakeholders at: www.virginmedia.com/about/cr/stakeholders.php

EXTERNAL STAKEHOLDERS

Stakeholder	Interest	Influence
Customers	Quality products Value for money	Choice (whether or not to buy) Influence products and services company provides Recommendations to friends and family
Banks and lenders	Financial stability of organisation Want to ensure existing customers (organisations) can pay back loans Want to ensure that those applying for loans have sufficient funds to pay them back	Can grant or withhold loans Set loan interest rates Request repayment of loans if the organisation's ability to make repayments is in doubt
Donors (for charities)	Corporate donors will want the charity to be successful May be good for public relations	May or may not donate Donors of large amounts may specify how the money should be used
Suppliers and creditors	Want organisation to be successful (to get repeat business) Depend on organisations for survival	Prices (they can change them) Credit periods Discounts offered
Taxpayers	In publicly funded bodies Want to ensure taxes used effectively	Voting for political parties (at national and local government elections)
Local community	Employment opportunities Increased wealth in the area Environmental factors (for example, pollution and noise)	Petitions Complaints to local authority
Central government	Provide jobs Generate wealth Provide taxes (Inland Revenue)	Legislation Economic policies Interest rates
Local government	Revenue from business rates Improves image if successful businesses in area Services for schools, government targets, justify budget spending	Granting or not granting licences Allocation of funding from council budgets Operational policies for services

DON'T FORGET

Stakeholders have an interest in the **success** of a business.

LET'S THINK ABOUT THIS

1 Learning and Teaching Scotland (LT Scotland) provides advice, support, resources and staff development to the education community in Scotland. Who are its main stakeholders? What is their interest in LT Scotland? What influence could they have on LT Scotland? www.ltscotland.org.uk/

2 Who do you think the stakeholders of the Food Standards Agency are? Take a look at their website. www.food.gov.uk/

SOURCES OF ASSISTANCE AND FINANCE

SOURCES OF ASSISTANCE

Scottish Government

The Scottish Government has a range of initiatives to encourage and support businesses – see www.scotland.gov.uk/Topics/Business-Industry/support for details.

Scottish Enterprise including Highlands and Islands Enterprise

- government-funded
- advice for business start-ups
- help existing companies grow
- offer advice and training courses, and provide contacts
- assist with gaining grants and funding
- promote exporting

Business Gateway

- provides information on finance, grants, taxation, health and safety, IT and e-business, sales and marketing

Careers Scotland

- part of Skills Development Scotland
- provides assistance with recruitment and training
- source of information on local labour market
- gives advice on employment law

Scottish Chamber of Commerce

- businesses can become members of this organisation
- seminars on business topics
- networking opportunities
- encourage exporting and international trade

European Union

- provides a range of grants

HM Revenue and Customs

- taxation matters

Lawyers and accountants

- legal and financial advice

Trade associations

- business-specific advice

The Prince's Scottish Youth Business Trust (PSYBT)

- charity providing low cost loans and grants to young people aged 18-25 interested in starting a business in Scotland. PSYBT also provide business mentoring, training and professional advice.

Banks

- source of finance (loan/overdraft)
- advice on financial planning
- drawing up a business plan

Local authorities

- locating premises
- local planning matters
- loans and grants
- subsidised premises

 DON'T FORGET

Organisations may use several different sources of assistance.

 You can find out more about the Business Gateway and The Prince's Scottish Youth Business Trust at the following websites: www.bgateway.com/ and www.psybt.org.uk/

 DON'T FORGET

Questions about sources of finance are often part of a more general question on other areas of finance; see page 72.

ADVANTAGES AND DISADVANTAGES OF FINANCE OPTIONS

Sources of finance were summarised on page 9.

 Read through (and complete the activities) on sources of finance at: www.bized.co.uk/educators/level2/finance/lesson/sources1.htm

contd

ADVANTAGES AND DISADVANTAGES OF FINANCE OPTIONS contd

Short-term		Medium-term		Long-term	
Advantages	Disadvantages	Advantages	Disadvantages	Advantages	Disadvantages
Bank overdraft: an amount of money can be withdrawn or used for payments (up to an agreed limit).		**Bank loan:** a specific amount of money borrowed over an agreed period for a specific purpose.		**Owner's savings:** savings built up, by the business owner, that can be used in the business.	
Borrow more than you have saved – to agreed limit. Easy to arrange. Relatively cheap.	Expensive over time. If limit exceeded, it may be withdrawn and expensive charges incurred.	Repaid in instalments. Budgeting and planning easier.	Often higher interest rates for small businesses.	Reduces amount you have to borrow. You keep control.	Owner's capital at risk if business fails. Difficult to withdraw capital again.
Trade credit: credit from one business to another.		**Leasing:** rent vehicles or equipment.		**Share issue:** when new shares are sold to raise capital.	
Buy goods now and pay for them later. Useful when cash flow is a problem.	No discount for prompt payment. If you don't pay when agreed, creditor might not do business with you again.	Cheaper than buying in short term. Equipment changed when outdated.	Business doesn't own equipment. Rental charges build up over time – could be more expensive than buying.	Limited liability and annual dividend for shareholders. Large sums can be raised. Doesn't need to be repaid.	Issuing shares can be expensive. Difficult to decide on selling price of shares.
Factoring: factor buys your invoices from you (usually for less than full value).		**Hire purchase:** deposit paid, and remainder paid in instalments.		**Debentures:** loans from individuals and/or other companies.	
Improves cash flow. Factor chases unpaid invoices, saving company time and money.	Factors only want large invoices/large quantities. Business doesn't get full amount of invoice.	Cost is spread. Equipment owned by company once paid up.	Goods owned by finance company until last instalment paid. Expensive form of borrowing.	Used by plcs. Debenture-holders receive fixed interest over loan period – recover loan at end. Raises large amounts.	Interest must be paid even if business making a loss. Debenture-holders have right to sell assets, so loan repaid if business fails.
Grant: central government, EU, LEC or Prince's Trust.				**Venture capital:** from venture capitalists.	
New business incentive – particularly in areas of high unemployment.	One-off payment – not usually repeated.			Often provide finance when banks decide it is too risky.	Usually only interested in very large loans. Fees often high. May want part-ownership in exchange.
Retained profits: last year's profits used to purchase assets.					
Self-reliant.	Could slow growth.				

LET'S THINK ABOUT THIS

In order to gain finance from banks, local authorities or other organisations, businesses are often required to prepare and produce a business plan. Search for examples of business plans on the internet and identify the main areas that should be included.

METHODS OF GROWTH

Organisations can grow **internally** – by opening new sales outlets, hiring additional staff or developing new products. **External** growth happens when one company combines with another. This can take the form of **integration** with another organisation through a **merger** or a **takeover**.

INTEGRATION

Method	Meaning	Potential benefits
Horizontal integration	Companies producing the same type of product, or same service, combine.	<ul><li>economies of scale/reduce unit cost of products</li><li>can dominate the market as a larger single organisation</li><li>reduction in competition may allow higher prices to be charged</li></ul>
Vertical integration	Companies at different stages in the same industry combine (for example, a clothes manufacturer and retail outlet).	<ul><li>profits are increased by cutting out the 'middleman'</li><li>stock can be cheaper due to backward integration</li><li>guaranteed source of supplies and prices of stock</li><li>reduction in costs</li></ul>
Conglomerate (diversification) integration	Companies in different businesses merge.	<ul><li>reduces the risk of business failure, as the income comes from a variety of areas – if one does poorly one year, then others may help to carry it</li><li>new opportunities</li><li>larger, more financially secure business</li></ul>

DECISIONS THAT CAN LEAD TO GROWTH

Open new branches	to expand the number of outlets for the product and increase customer numbers and sales
Introduce internet shopping	to target a wider (perhaps even international) customer base and attract new customers/increase sales
Target new market segments	to widen the appeal of the product and attract new customers/increase sales
Launch a new range of products	to refresh the company's image and encourage new or returning customers
Vertical integration (with a company at a different point in the supply chain)	to control the supplier or outlet
Horizontal integration (with a company at the same point in the supply chain)	to dominate the market – this will eliminate some competition and increase the product range/number of outlets/customer base

DON'T FORGET

Some exam questions may require knowledge of different parts of the syllabus. For example, a question may ask for examples of decisions that could lead to growth. You could answer the question with examples of integration **and** product or marketing suggestions.

OTHER KEY TERMS

De-integration

- Business cuts back on, or sells, minor areas of the business.
- Allows concentration on core areas.
- Provides money from sale of less profitable areas.

De-merger

- Business splits into two separate organisations.
- Concentrates efforts on core activities.
- Cuts costs to make it more efficient.

Divestment

- Business sells its assets or a subsidiary to raise finance.

Asset-stripping

- Business buys another, then gradually sells off the profitable sections and closes down the loss-making sections.

Contracting out/outsourcing

- Business hires another firm to conduct some of its services.
- Normally occurs if the business does not have the skills, staff or equipment to do the task itself.
- For example, some companies contract out their IT support, catering, cleaning, delivery or accountancy.

Management buy-out

- Managers buy the business they work for from the current owners.
- Managers then own the business.
- This happens when managers want to keep their jobs and make the firm more efficient.
- Current owners might want to sell the business to raise money.

Management buy-in

- Group of managers outside the company takes over and runs the business.

 Look at this website for definitions of a wide range of business terms:
http://moneyterms.co.uk/

LET'S THINK ABOUT THIS

AG Barr, makers of Irn Bru, bought Rubicon in 2008. Read the article at the link below and identify examples of integration, acquisition, financing, impact on shares and economies of scale.

www.theherald.co.uk/business/news/display.var.2418367.0.AG_Barr_acquires_Groupe_Rubicon.php

BUSINESS AS A DYNAMIC ACTIVITY

There are many internal and external factors that can influence the performance of a business.

INTERNAL FACTORS

Finance available	To expand business, buy new equipment, train staff.
Ability of staff	A skilled workforce will be more efficient and make fewer mistakes.
Information available	Good information is essential for good decision-making.
ICT available	Good use of ICT can improve efficiency and reduce costs.
Ability of management	Poor managers will make bad decisions.
Changes in costs	Increased salary bills or running costs mean that less money is available for other areas.

EXTERNAL FACTORS

The external factors are those that the business can do little or nothing to influence. It is crucial that the business is aware of what is happening externally, so that it can react in a way that minimises any potential damage to its success.

P	Political factors	UK and EU laws. Political decisions by local and national government. Taxation rates. Terrorism.
E	Economic factors	Inflation (increased prices or costs). Exchange rates (value of one currency against another – can affect imports/exports and tourism). Interest rates (can affect the cost of loans). Recession (a slowdown in the economy = fall in demand). Boom period (an upturn in the economy = increase in demand). Unemployment (less money for people to spend).
S	Social factors	Demographic changes (the rise or fall in population). Socio-cultural changes (population distribution, age or family size). Increased number of women working.
T	Technological factors	New technology used for: • communication (for example, e-mail and internet) • marketing and sales (for example, E-commerce and internet) • production (for example, CAD/CAM).
E	Environmental factors	Floods, storms, pollution, noise. Changing weather patterns. Environmental issues.
C	Competitive factors	Domestic and foreign competition. Actions of competitors may result in an organisation having to change the way it operates.

DON'T FORGET

As well as being able to identify and describe the internal and external influences, you must also be able to say what effect they might have on an organisation.

This link has more examples of PEST analysis:
www.thetimes100.co.uk/theory/theory--pest-analysis--166.php

BUSINESS ENVIRONMENT

The business environment is constantly changing and evolving. In recent years, this has resulted in the following trends.

Multinationals	Increasingly significant.
	Expanding into emerging economies.
	Dominating the marketplace with their global brands (for example, Coca-Cola, McDonald's).
	Deter competition.
Publicly-funded organisations becoming more business-orientated	Accountable to government and taxpayer.
	In charge of own finances.
	Have to operate within budgets.
	Business managers are used to control organisation.
	Adopting business practices (outsourcing, appraisal).
A significant contribution from SMEs (Small and Medium Enterprises)	97 per cent of companies in Scotland are SMEs.
	Estimated two thirds of workforce work for companies with fewer than 100 employees.
	E-commerce has helped SMEs find markets for their products/ services.
	Some have benefited from outsourcing by larger organisations.
	Entrepreneurship has been encouraged.
	Increasing number of over-50s starting up their own business.
Downsizing	Reduction in staffing levels to help cut costs and make company more competitive.
Franchising	The number of franchise outlets has grown in recent years.

 Test your knowledge of external factors with the Shell quiz on External Environment at: www.thetimes100.co.uk/revision/index.php

LET'S THINK ABOUT THIS

Companies that have recently failed include Woolworths, Zavvi and Fopp. Two of these have now reopened. Read the articles on the websites below. Also see the case study on Fopp in Section 1 of the 2009 Higher Business Management paper.

Why do you think the Wellworths store might have success where Woolworths failed? Why do you think Fopp has been saved by HMV in these locations?

www.thisismoney.co.uk/news/article.html?in_article_id=474912&in_page_id=2

www.foppreturns.com/

BUSINESS INFORMATION

DATA AND INFORMATION

You will often hear the terms **data** and **information** used when discussing business information. The distinction between the two is quite clear:

Data is a collection of raw facts and figures that has been brought together in an organised way. The data is then processed to produce something more meaningful.

Information is data that has been processed to make it meaningful to the user. This information is used to assist in the decision-making process.

Data ▷ Process ▷ Information

SOURCES OF BUSINESS INFORMATION

You should know that there are **four sources of information**. The information source tells you where the information has come from.

Primary

Primary information is created by the organisation; for example, information collected in a questionnaire or observed by staff.

Strengths	Weaknesses
It has been gathered for a specific purpose and should be correct.	It may cost a lot to collect, especially if a market-research company has been used.
It can be kept private.	The information may be flawed – it may have used too small a sample, or leading questions.
It is probably up to date.	It can be time-consuming and difficult to collect.
You know it comes from a reliable source.	Those providing the information may have lied.
	The researcher may be biased.

Secondary

Secondary information is gathered from an existing source; for example, from government reports, newspapers or the internet.

Strengths	Weaknesses
It can be easy to access.	The information has been gathered for a certain purpose and may not be relevant to another.
It can be inexpensive to collect.	It could be out of date.
There is a wide variety of potential sources.	The author who created it may have been biased.
	If it is available to you, it is also available to your competitors.

contd

SOURCES OF BUSINESS INFORMATION contd

Internal

This information is collected from within the organisation; for example, from computer files or company reports.

Strengths	Weaknesses
A bank of accurate information can be built up over a number of years.	The cost of setting up and producing the information may be high.
Realistic targets can be set on the basis of past performance.	New organisations have little internal information to access.
It is easy to access.	Records need to be kept accurately and updated regularly.

External

This information is gathered from outside the organisation; for example, from market research, from newspapers or from competitors' annual reports.

Strengths	Weaknesses
Potentially good source of information about PESTEC factors.	It may be time-consuming to collect.
It is inexpensive and easy to get hold of.	It may be out of date.
It is probably up to date.	It could be unreliable or biased.
	It is also available to competitors.

DON'T FORGET

Information that the business has collected itself is often more reliable than that collected from other sources. However, it can be expensive to collect.

For a useful summary of information in business, visit:
http://tutor2u.net/business/ict/intro_business_information.htm

You will find some good examples of information from both internal and external sources at: http://tutor2u.net/business/ict/intro_information_sources.htm

LET'S THINK ABOUT THIS

Read this quote taken from the website below. What type of information is this for the executive? What are the advantages of using the internet as a source, rather than, for example, a newspaper or company report?

'The most important source of business information for senior executives around the world is the web. A recent study by Forbes.com and Gartner has announced that executives are increasingly using the internet to gain information, while newspapers continue to decline in importance.'

www.realnet.co.uk/news/2008/7/senior-executives-use-the-web-for-business-information

TYPES AND CHARACTERISTICS OF INFORMATION

TYPES OF INFORMATION

DON'T FORGET

Make sure you know the difference between **sources** and **types** of information. Remember that there are **four** **sources** and **seven types**.

You need to be able to discuss the **seven types of information**.

Written

- used to confirm verbal messages
- good for information that needs to be kept
- easy to collect
- you can refer back to it to check details
- examples: reports, letters, memos, minutes, agendas, e-mails, case studies and newsletters

Oral

- mainly used for passing on simple instructions and advice
- informal/formal discussions (formal are usually confirmed in writing)
- main problems: can be easily forgotten or misinterpreted
- can be recorded

Pictorial

- used to add interest or to emphasise something
- useful when passing on information that is easy to remember
- might not always be easy to find a suitable picture

Graphical

- graphs and charts; for example, pictographs, bar graphs, line graphs
- good for displaying numerical data (particularly when used to show trends or comparisons)
- usually produced from spreadsheet data

Numerical

- usually displayed in spreadsheets and tables
- enables staff to perform calculations using the data
- analysis of the information can help managers to make decisions
- can be used in a spreadsheet to make financial predictions and carry out 'what-if' analysis

Quantitative – think quantity

- information that can be measured; for example, number of items sold, percentage sales increase
- normally expressed numerically

Qualitative – think quality

- descriptive information that is expressed in words
- involves judgements or opinions (something is good or bad, or better/worse than it was)
- often used in surveys to find out what customers think of services or products
- can be difficult to analyse

This case study on the Food Standards Agency discusses how they conducted market research using primary, secondary, qualitative and quantitative research techniques to help them meet the expectations of their stakeholders. www.thetimes100.co.uk/case-study--market-research-consumer-protection--116-300-3.php

DON'T FORGET

Not just **any** information will do – it needs to be **good** information. Acting on the wrong information can lead to bad decisions.

CHARACTERISTICS OF GOOD INFORMATION

Information, however you collect or present it, is of no use unless it is fit for purpose. This means that it must be what the user needs to do the job and/or to make decisions. It must be presented in a way that is clear and makes sense. Good decisions cannot be made using bad information. Good information has the following characteristics:

Getting the right information at the right time can be a balancing act. Certain characteristics of good information can sometimes conflict:

- It has to be **accurate and reliable**, but you need it by a **specific time**.
- It has to be **complete**, but also **concise**.
- It has to be **appropriate** to the task, but you want to gather it in a **cost-effective** way.

When collecting and presenting information, it is essential to get the timing and planning right if you want to have the information you need when you need it.

You can read a summary of what makes good-quality business information here: http://tutor2u.net/business/ict/intro_information_qualities.htm

LET'S THINK ABOUT THIS

Read the statement below, taken from page 3 of a case study on the Food Standards Agency. Considering the role of the FSA, do you think this is wise? Why? What do you think the advantages and disadvantages of this approach are?
'FSA does not make decisions or rely solely on research by third parties, unless its own research supports the findings.'
www.thetimes100.co.uk/case-study--market-research-consumer-protection--116-300-3.php

USE OF INFORMATION IN BUSINESS

Business information can be put to a variety of uses, not just in decision-making.

MONITORING AND CONTROLLING THE BUSINESS

Information is used to:

- check progress, so that corrective action can be taken if necessary
- monitor performance against targets so that progress can be assessed.

The types of information used to help monitor and control performance include departmental budgets, sales forecasts, sales records and production records. This information can be used to ensure that the business is running as planned.

DECISION-MAKING

Managers and business owners use information to help them make decisions. They have to decide:

- how to price their products
- when and where to advertise
- how much to pay their staff
- when to buy new plant and machinery
- whether or not to introduce new products.

They need good, **up-to-date** information to help ensure that they make good decisions in these areas. The wrong decision could have a disastrous effect on the company.

DON'T FORGET

Remember to revise examples of bad information and its consequences:
- Historical information might be out of date. If it doesn't reflect the current situation, it could result in bad decisions.
- Information that is biased can lead to poor decisions, as it doesn't give a balanced view.
- Incomplete information can result in bad decisions because it represents only part of the picture.

MEASURING PERFORMANCE

Managers need to know how their business is performing. They will do this by

- recording sales data and comparing it with targets
- recording production data and comparing it with their plans
- comparing how they are doing with previous years
- comparing how they are doing against their competitors.

They will then know if things are going well. If they are not, then managers will be better placed to decide on how they should deal with the situation.

IDENTIFYING NEW BUSINESS OPPORTUNITIES

Business is constantly changing, and managers must be aware of what is happening so that they can take advantage of it. There will always be new or changing opportunities – as long as you can spot them. To help them identify new business opportunities, managers could:

- conduct market research to find out what people want

- ask their existing customers what they want

- be aware of political changes that might affect their business (for example, many pubs started selling more food when the smoking ban was introduced; local producers sold more through farmers' markets when consumers were persuaded to reduce the 'air miles' of their food).

EVALUATING DECISIONS

Once a decision has been made and implemented, managers should go back and evaluate the decision to see whether or not it has had the desired effect. This could be achieved in a number of ways. They could check to see if:

- sales or profits had increased – by analysing sales figures, income and expenditure

- production quality or quantity had improved – by analysing output and production reports

- staff morale had improved – by speaking to staff, observing, analysing absenteeism reports, analysing staff turnover figures, issuing questionnaires, interviewing staff

- costs had reduced – by analysing accounts.

 Read the summary about the use of financial information in decision-making at the link below. You might find this interesting if you are thinking of becoming an accountant, but don't worry about the fact that it is specific to finance. It discusses using financial information to measure performance, help with forward planning and monitor activities – does this sound familiar?
www.thetimes100.co.uk/studies/view-summary--financial-information-decision-making--114--281.php

LET'S THINK ABOUT THIS

Read the article below. What kind of decision was this? What types of things would the managers have had to consider when making this decision? The decision was 'carefully evaluated'. What do you think would have been taken into consideration when evaluating the decision?

Jobs cut as CD factory shuts down

A factory in Lancashire which claims to be the largest CD manufacturing facility in the UK is to close down with the loss of 260 jobs.

EDC Blackburn is to shut in December, its owners have announced, with production moving to Hannover, Germany.

EDC on Phillips Road has been making discs there since the mid-1980s and produces the CD for the winner of ITV1's *The X Factor*.

The firm's chief executive said the closure decision was 'not an easy one'.

The decision was a result of a 'strategic review process' over the last two years, EDC said.

Robert Chapman, EDC chief executive officer, said: 'This decision was carefully evaluated, and not an easy one for EDC to make. It in no way reflects upon the performance or quality of work undertaken by EDC's UK employees.'

BBC News, 31 March 2009

ICT IN BUSINESS

USES OF ICT (INFORMATION AND COMMUNICATIONS TECHNOLOGIES)

The main uses of ICT in business are:

- **E-mail** (internal and external) – allows staff to communicate quickly and cheaply at a time that suits them.
- **Creation and manipulation of text and data** – using various software packages.
- **Videoconferencing** – to help save on travel costs and time.
- **File-sharing** – to reduce duplication of data and the use of out-of-date data.
- **E-commerce** – to widen marketing opportunities. This area has grown very quickly in recent years. Companies can take orders around the clock and from anywhere in the world. They don't even need to have expensive premises or a shop front on the high street.
- **Internet** – for information-gathering, marketing or travel arrangements.
- **Computer-Based Training (CBT)** – to help keep staff skills up to date in a cost-effective and flexible way. The training package is often supplied on CD or DVD, or it may be available over the internet.
- **Computer-Aided Manufacture (CAM)** – to automate the manufacture of goods, such as cars.

HARDWARE AND SOFTWARE

Hardware is a term used to refer to computer systems (for example, mainframes, desktop PCs, laptops or handheld devices), networking equipment (for example, cables, routers and servers) and printers, scanners, wireless hotspots and web cams.

Networks can be LANs (Local Area Networks) or WANs (Wide Area Networks). LANs link up equipment in the same building, site or location, whereas WANs are used to connect computers over the country, continent or globe. Networks enable companies to benefit from file-sharing and e-mail.

Software is a term used to refer to operating systems such as Windows®, as well as network software (required to link computers together to form a network). Software also refers to a wide range of applications (such as those used for word-processing, spreadsheets, accounts, e-mail, databases, desk-top publishing, videoconferencing, point-of-sale, presentation graphics and browsing the internet). Most business users interact with their computer hardware through software.

DON'T FORGET

E-commerce is the buying and selling of goods and services via the internet.

You should be aware of the different types of ICT commonly used in business. See the link below to revise some of them.
www.bbc.co.uk/schools/gcsebitesize/business/people/ictrev1.shtml

Look up the link below for an overview of changing work patterns that are a direct result of increased use of ICT by businesses.
www.bbc.co.uk/schools/gcsebitesize/ict/implications/2workpatternsrev1.shtml

Look up this link for some ideas on what companies should consider when purchasing or upgrading their hardware and/or software.
www.bbc.co.uk/schools/gcsebitesize/ict/software/7evaluationrev1.shtml

COSTS AND BENEFITS OF ICT

It is generally accepted that the benefits of ICT outweigh the costs. But the costs are considerable and should not be ignored or underestimated.

Benefits of ICT	Costs of ICT
Reduced waste – information can be accessed electronically, reducing the need to print. This can help the company meet its 'green' targets.	Bad feelings between management and workers when new equipment and systems are introduced.
ICT increases productivity, as information can be created, analysed and found more quickly.	The costs of development, installation, maintenance, redundancy payments and retraining can be high.
Improved accuracy. As long as you put the correct information in, and use the correct tools to analyse it, fewer errors will be made.	Staff need retraining and 'up-skilling' regularly. This can be difficult if the new skills are not easily acquired by those in the old jobs.
More work can be achieved using fewer people.	'De-skilling' of workers can reduce staff motivation. Tasks that were once highly skilled (such as typesetting newspapers and other publications) can now be done relatively easily using applications such as DTP.
Consistent production quality – CAM ensures that products are consistently produced within set limits.	ICT breakdowns can cause stoppages in production and inconvenience. Tesco were unable to take money across the country when their tills stopped working after an IT upgrade. This cost a lot in lost income, not to mention upsetting their customers.
Increases access to information. A vast amount of information can be accessed with a few keystrokes, and that information could be anywhere in the world.	Data can be vulnerable and corrupted by viruses, industrial espionage and network failure.
Saves money – ICT is often more reliable than manual labour and less expensive.	Technical support is required.
Improves communication and decision-making – people can communicate very quickly over long distances, getting up-to-date information as soon as it is available. This helps decision-making.	Recovery plans need to be put in place in case of serious problems (for example, if equipment is damaged by flood or fire).
Fewer workplace accidents occur as working conditions are improved with new technology. People can work from their desks and don't have to travel to get information or carry it back. The work isn't usually dangerous – unlike some earlier trades and professions.	

DON'T FORGET

There are costs as well as benefits of ICT – make sure you know them.

LET'S THINK ABOUT THIS

Read the article at the link below, which gives guidelines on how to get the most from IT in a business. Think about your own experiences of ICT, and give examples of how it affects your normal daily life.

www.businesslink.gov.uk/bdotg/action/detail?type=CASE%20STUDIES&itemId=1075070442

EFFECTS OF ICT ON STAFF AND THE ORGANISATION

The introduction or increase in the use of ICT by an organisation will usually have some effect on current staff and the organisation.

EFFECTS ON STAFF

The main effects on staff are:

- Fewer staff members needed – ICT usually results in greater productivity, so more work can be done by fewer people. This can result in lowered staff morale and possible industrial action.
- Retraining/'up-skilling' – staff who remain with the company will often need training to use the new equipment and work with new procedures.
- Older staff may feel unable to cope with the changes.
- Customer contact often changes. The use of websites and call centres reduces the amount of personal contact between staff and customers.
- There is less personal contact between staff as e-mail replaces some meetings.
- Working practices may change – many jobs can be done from home with the right ICT equipment.

EFFECTS ON THE ORGANISATION

The main effects on the organisation are:

- ICT and improved communication between staff can lead to decentralisation, with more decisions being taken away from head office.
- Videoconferencing and e-mail allow staff to communicate easily, even when they are far apart.
- New departments may emerge (for example, Web Team or E-commerce).
- If fewer staff are required, de-layering and redundancies may occur, and savings are made as the wages bill is reduced.
- If fewer staff are required, managers will be responsible for fewer individuals, leading to a reduced span of control.

DON'T FORGET

Increased use of ICT can result in staff anxiety. Staff members may need to be retrained or may find that their jobs change or disappear.

ICT has made it feasible for staff to work successfully – without going to the office. But it isn't just a case of sending someone home with a laptop! Get some hints and tips on how to ensure the success of remote working at: http://insight.bt.com/articles/Remote-working-hints-and-tips/

CURRENT LEGISLATION

The main piece of legislation that you should be familiar with is the **Data Protection Act 1998**. The act lays down rules about how organisations can use the personal data they hold on individuals. The data covered by the act is usually held on computers, but could also be stored in paper filing systems. Personal data is any data that can be used to identify a **living individual**.

contd

CURRENT LEGISLATION contd

Any record that displays names and addresses – customer records, membership records, student records, staff records – is covered by the act.

Companies that hold this type of data must be registered with the **Information Commissioner**. When registering, they must state the **purpose** of holding the data. Individuals have the right to access any information stored about them, and they can challenge it and claim compensation if it is inaccurate.

There are eight data-protection principles:

You should be familiar with the **Computer Misuse Act (1990)**. This act makes it an offence to:

1 access information on a computer without permission; for example, to look at someone else's files

2 access information on a computer without permission **with the intention** of committing further criminal offences; for example, to hack into a computer to change an exam mark

3 alter computer data without permission; for example, to change data or to write a virus that will destroy someone else's data.

DON'T FORGET

The Data Protection Act was introduced for two reasons: first, to control the way organisations can use the data that they hold, and second, to give certain legal rights to people whose information is stored.

For more information on the Data Protection Act, visit:
www.bbc.co.uk/schools/gcsebitesize/ict/legal/0dataprotectionactrev1.shtml

For more information on the Computer Misuse Act, visit:
www.bbc.co.uk/schools/gcsebitesize/ict/legal/1dataandcomputermisuserev1.shtml

LET'S THINK ABOUT THIS

Read the articles on the websites below. In what way were these Data Protection issues?

http://news.bbc.co.uk/1/hi/scotland/south_of_scotland/7584048.stm

http://news.bbc.co.uk/1/hi/uk_politics/7472814.stm

DECISION-MAKING IN BUSINESS

A decision is a choice between two or more alternatives. If you have only one choice, then you have no decision to make.

THE NATURE OF DECISION

Decision-making lies at the heart of business activity. Organisations must make decisions in order to achieve their objectives. Decision-making involves choosing a course of action from the different options available.

TYPES OF DECISION: STRATEGIC, TACTICAL AND OPERATIONAL

There are three types of decisions that organisations need to make. You must be able to name them, list their main features and be able to **give examples** of the types of decision taken at each level.

Strategic
- Made by senior management
- Long term decisions that set out the aims of the organisation
- Define the organisation's overall purpose and direction

Tactical
- Made by middle-level management
- Set out the objectives of the organisation
- Short-medium-term decisions on how to achieve strategic decisions

Operational
- Made by lower-level management
- Short-term, day-to-day, routine decisions

Level	Examples of decisions
Strategic	Whether to take over Company A or Company B; whether or not to open a factory overseas; how much the company should grow over a given period; whether or not to move into a new market segment.
Tactical	How many extra staff members to recruit; what products to develop for a new market; where a new retail outlet should be; how to cut staff costs.
Operational	Where to order supplies; what delivery company to use; how to reorganise staff to cover for sickness.

A **mission statement** is a written summary of the strategic objectives of the company. It is often published once senior management have decided on the organisation's objectives. It lets staff, customers and suppliers know what these are. The mission statement is often displayed on a poster in a company's reception area. It can help to give staff a sense of direction – they know what the company is trying to achieve.

The presentation at the link below highlights many of the key features of business decision-making.
http://insightory.com/view/1040//business_enterprise:_decision_making

ROLE OF MANAGERS

Managers must be able to make good decisions based on the available information. They must also be able to work under pressure, analyse information, negotiate and communicate decisions to staff. Here is a summary of the skills required by a manager:

Think about any manager you know – from a football manager to the manager in your local supermarket. Think about what they do. Can you recognise the skills listed above in what they do?

DON'T FORGET

Managers not only make decisions, they also **evaluate** them to check that their decisions are having the desired effect. See page 36.

DON'T FORGET

Senior managers have a lot of experience and knowledge of their marketplace. They know about the competition, as well as their own company, and know what type of support they can get. This knowledge and experience is useful when making strategic decisions.

 Read a summary of a manager's roles and responsibilities at
www.about-personal-growth.com/managers.html

LET'S THINK ABOUT THIS

1 The Virgin Group has established businesses in many different sectors (see www.virgin.com/). Find examples of some recent business decisions taken by Virgin. Classify each decision you find – is it strategic, tactical or operational? Give a reason for your answer.

2 The publisher Bloomsbury made a very good business decision in 1995–96. What was it? What type of decision was this, and what was the overall effect on Bloomsbury?

DECISION-MAKING MODELS

Decision-making can be centralised or decentralised. You should be able to discuss the advantages and disadvantages of each. For example, for decentralised decision-making:

Advantages	Disadvantages
Increased staff motivation (which could result in productivity improvements).	Not all managers are keen to be involved in decision-making (some are more comfortable monitoring and controlling).
More flexible staff (as they feel involved in what is happening).	Managers who do like making decisions may be unwilling to give up this responsibility.
Improved communication (as there are fewer managers, and decisions are being taken closer to the workforce).	Training (which could be expensive) may be required to enable staff to make effective decisions.
Decisions are taken more quickly.	
More ideas emerge to help solve problems as more people are involved.	

POGADSCIE

Decision-making models are tools that managers can use to help them solve problems and make decisions. You should know the nine-step model **POGADSCIE**.

	Step	What it means
P	Identify the **P**roblem	Be clear about what the problem is, and write it down so that you can refer back to it.
O	Identify the **O**bjectives	Be clear about what you want to achieve by fixing the problem.
G	**G**ather information	Find out as much as you can about the problem. Speak to staff, collect minutes and reports, get hold of spreadsheets, collect customer comments and so on.
A	**A**nalyse the information	Study the information so that you have a clear picture of the problem.
D	**D**evise alternative solutions	Come up with possible solutions; for example, train staff, employ more staff, make more effective use of ICT, change suppliers.
S	**S**elect from alternatives	Select the best solution(s) from those identified.
C	**C**ommunicate the decision	Let people know what is going to be done.
I	**I**mplement the decision	Carry out the chosen solution(s).
E	**E**valuate the effectiveness of the decision and the influence of ICT	You could ask staff or customers (perhaps by using interviews or questionnaires, analysing sales and profit data, monitoring staff absenteeism and morale or analysing production figures).

DON'T FORGET

Decision-making models help managers to analyse a problem so that they can make an objective, or unbiased, decision.

DON'T FORGET

SWOT = strengths, weaknesses, opportunities, threats.

STRENGTHS, WEAKNESSES, OPPORTUNITIES, THREATS (SWOT) ANALYSIS

SWOT analysis is used in the **POG** part of POGADSCIE: identifying the problem, identifying the objectives, gathering the information.

DEVELOPMENT OF SWOT ANALYSIS

Decisions are effective if the following points are analysed and considered:

Strengths	Weaknesses
Internal areas or activities.	Internal areas or activities.
Areas where the organisation performs well.	Areas where the organisation performs poorly.
Opportunities	**Threats**
External areas or activities.	External areas or activities.
Areas that the organisation could be profitably involved with in the future.	Areas that could cause problems (competitors, economic forces).

OTHER DECISION-MAKING TECHNIQUES

Thought showers – a group of people come up with as many ideas as possible in a short period of time. Each idea is then discussed with a view to identifying feasible solutions.

PEST analysis – this is similar to SWOT, but political, economic, social and technological factors are identified. Strategies can then be developed to deal with each.

AREAS FOR ANALYSIS

Internal areas for analysis

1 Finance (for example, an opportunity to invest, or make an acquisition; a potential partnership).

2 Human resources.

3 Management styles and structures.

4 Operations and productions (for example, outsourcing a service, activity or resource).

5 Organisational structure.

6 Products.

7 Sales and marketing (for example, a method of sales distribution, a product or a brand).

8 Technology (for example, whether to upgrade a system, whether to invest in a new CRM system).

9 A business idea.

10 A strategic option (for example, entering a new market or launching a new product).

External areas for analysis

1 Competitors (for example, their position in the market or commercial viability)

2 Consumer tastes.

3 Economic climate.

4 Environmental changes.

5 Political situation.

6 Social and demographic changes.

7 Suppliers (for example, changing a supplier).

8 Technological changes.

Try the business-studies quiz at the link below. You can visit it throughout your revision (a lot of the syllabus is covered) – and it's fun!
www.bbc.co.uk/schools/gcsebitesize/games/lostarmy/index.shtml

LET'S THINK ABOUT THIS

Early in 2009, drinks giant Diageo revealed that it planned to scale down its business activities in Scotland as part of a global restructuring exercise (resulting in hundreds of job losses). Read the articles at the link below. What PEST factors would Diageo have taken into consideration when making this decision?

http://thescotsman.scotsman.com/newsfront.aspx?sectionid=16866&lsTopic=1

CONCLUSIONS, ADVANTAGES AND DISADVANTAGES

As well as knowing which decision-making models can be used, you also need to be able to discuss:

- what they tell you
- the advantages and disadvantages of using a certain model.

We summarised the meaning of **POGADSCIE** on page 36.

DRAWING CONCLUSIONS FROM A SWOT ANALYSIS

A SWOT analysis is used to:

DON'T FORGET

Exam questions might ask you to:
- **explain** how structured models can help with decision-making
- **justify** the use of structured models **or**
- **discuss** the advantages and disadvantages of using structured models.

Make sure you read the question carefully; don't just say what **POGADSCIE** and **SWOT** stand for.

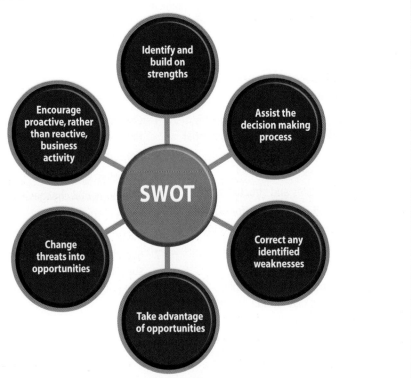

Identify and build on strengths

Assist the decision making process

Correct any identified weaknesses

Take advantage of opportunities

Change threats into opportunities

Encourage proactive, rather than reactive, business activity

SWOT

You will find a useful summary of SWOT at:
http://tutor2u.net/business/strategy/SWOT_analysis.htm

ADVANTAGES AND DISADVANTAGES OF USING STRUCTURED MODELS

Structured models help managers to analyse problems and reach decisions objectively. However, this approach can be time-consuming, and it might be difficult to choose from a range of different solutions.

The advantages and disadvantages of using structured models are given below.

Advantages	Disadvantages
No hasty decisions are made.	Time-consuming.
Time is taken to gather information and analyse decisions.	Slows down decision-making process.
Time is taken to consider internal and external effects and influences.	Can be difficult to choose from range of options.
Decisions are based on relevant knowledge of facts.	Structured process can stifle creativity.
Time is taken to develop alternative solutions.	
Logical process is followed (better ideas developed).	
Decision is evaluated after implementation.	

DON'T FORGET

If you use bullet points when giving your answer, expand each point fully to explain what you mean. You will need to give more than a list.

LET'S THINK ABOUT THIS

Look up http://www.marketingteacher.com/

Scroll down the page until you reach the SWOT analysis links under the heading 'What SWOT analysis do you want to study?' Choose a couple, and look carefully at the strengths, weaknesses, opportunities and threats identified.

You will find a SWOT analysis template at www.businessballs.com/free_SWOT_analysis_template.pdf

Using the SWOT analysis template to help you, analyse your post-school plans. What are you hoping to do?

1 What strengths do you have that could help you get there?

2 What opportunities are there to help you reach your goal?

3 Do you have any weaknesses that you need to be aware of and try to overcome?

4 What threats are lurking that might prevent you from being successful?

Ask a friend to look at your SWOT analysis with you. Do they disagree with any of it? Can they think of anything you have forgotten?

OTHER INFLUENCES ON DECISION-MAKING

Effective decision-making can be difficult for a variety of reasons. The experience of the manager, the quality of information available and internal and external constraints can all have an effect. Some of the things that can affect the quality of a decision include:

INTERNAL CONSTRAINTS

1 Finance – the company may not be able to afford the best solution.

2 Existing company policy – some options may go against company policy, so have to be discounted.

3 Staff can resist change and sabotage attempts to implement some decisions.

4 Lack of appropriate technology.

5 Decision-making staff may

- have limited ideas
- be unable to handle stressful and complex situations or decisions
- have little opportunity to consult, resulting in poor decisions
- be indecisive and make poor decisions.

6 An overpowering managing director may overturn or veto decisions that are made by other managers.

DON'T FORGET

There are several factors that can affect the quality of decision-making.

EXTERNAL CONSTRAINTS

1 Political factors – laws passed by UK and EU governments.

2 Economic changes – recession.

3 Social factors.

4 Technological development.

5 Environmental changes.

6 Competitors' activities.

ICT AND DECISION-MAKING

ICT plays an important part in the decision-making process.

ICT	Use
Spreadsheets	'What-if' scenarios allow quick comparison of alternatives.
	Allow comparison of budget/sales figures to show how things really are, compared to plan.
	Allow analysis of data and show trends using charts and graphs.
Databases	Sales figures show what is selling well and what is not selling well.
	Allow analysis of staff data to show turnover and absences.
Project-management software	Helps managers to track the progress of a project.
	Used to help keep track of deadlines.
	Progress reports can be printed.
	Problems like schedule delays or exceeded costs can be identified and corrective action taken.
Management decision-making software	Allows analysis of internal company records.
Customer relationships management (CRM)	Collection and analysis of customer data (for example, product preferences and buying habits).
	Often linked to loyalty cards.
Computer-aided design software	Allows managers to make decisions on the design of a product without having to make a prototype.
E-mail and videoconferencing	Help to improve communication and decision-making.
Internet	Allows quick and cost-effective research for information (for example, into competitors' activities, other markets, international trade).
Mobile phones	Improve communication.

The article at the link below gives a summary of the main types of business software and its potential use.
http://tutor2u.net/business/ict/intro_what_is_ict.htm

LET'S THINK ABOUT THIS

Read the article at the link below. Identify five different types of software used by the company and say what they are used for.

www.bized.co.uk/compfact/kettleby/ket21.htm

FUNCTIONAL ACTIVITIES OF ORGANISATIONS

DON'T FORGET

The information covered on pages 42–49 is NOT assessed internally. However, it is assessed in the final exam, and therefore you will still need to read through it.

Businesses exist to make a profit. To do this, they need to carry out a range of activities. The number of departments within an organisation will depend on its size. Large companies that have diversified and have a number of different types of operation (for example, Virgin or Unilever) will be split into many different groupings.

ADVANTAGES AND DISADVANTAGES OF SPLITTING ORGANISATIONS

Splitting organisations into sections gives a number of advantages:

- more efficient use of resources and staff
- improved lateral communication between managers
- opportunities for teamwork
- clear line relationships

However, there are a few disadvantages:

- competition can arise between sections, making communication and decision-making difficult
- there can be resistance to change from one section, making it difficult for the others to function properly

FUNCTIONAL DEPARTMENTS

Use the following link to access the different functional divisions of the BBC: www.bbc.co.uk/info/running/bbcstructure/

Marketing

- promotion of goods and services
- selling goods and services – finding customers and selling the product
- communication with consumers – public relations, follow-up sales made, contact customers about new products in the hope of getting more sales

Product

Price

Target Market

Place

Promotion

FUNCTIONAL DEPARTMENTS contd

Human resources

- responsible for recruitment, selection, welfare and health and safety
- responsible for staff development
- help to manage staff

DON'T FORGET

You need to know how each functional department is dependent on, and interacts with, each of the others.

Finance

- maintain financial records – sales, purchases, salaries
- responsible for preparing final accounting statements
- negotiate and set budgets for departments

Operations

- responsible for purchasing and/or production of goods and services
- storage of materials and stock control
- getting the goods to the consumer (distribution)

Research and development

- work closely with marketing to ensure company can meet consumer needs and wants
- research the market, identify potential new products and services, develop products and services for market

Administration

- fulfil support function for the rest of the business
- help to ensure the flow of data and information to, and between, other functional areas

LET'S THINK ABOUT THIS

Think about large organisations like banks, supermarkets and high-street stores. Using either published financial accounts, or the internet, have a look at how they group their functional departments or divisions. Can you identify any trends?

GROUPING OF ACTIVITIES

By	Advantages	Disadvantages
FUNCTION **Business activities are grouped by sections or departments which reflect the functions of the business (for example, Sales and marketing).**	Good communications. Specialist staff grouped together, allowing expertise to be used to best effect. Good teamwork. Better decision-making. Career paths created within the department.	May need the involvement of more than one department to make decisions. Staff may be loyal to only one section. Staff may be resistant to change. Slow response to change.
PRODUCT/SERVICE **The business is grouped according to the products and services provided by the organisation.**	Employees become expert in product/service. Easy to see how the product is performing. Team can be responsive to any changes needed.	May be duplication of staff and resources. Potential for competition between sections.
PLACE/TERRITORY **The activities are grouped according to where the products are delivered.**	Employees get to know the local area and culture well. Minimises language problems – you can employ local people. Can respond to local consumer needs.	Changes in staff may mean extra training is required to help staff become familiar with the local environment. Extra administration could be costly. Duplication of staff and resources.
TECHNOLOGY **If the product/service relies heavily on a specific technology, then the activities may be based around the requirements of this technology.**	Upgrades to technology can be implemented quickly. Problems can be quickly sorted. Staff can become experts in their fields.	Expense in keeping up to date with technology. Need to recruit and train qualified staff or offer specialised training.
CUSTOMERS **Where the customer is of critical importance to the business, activities will be grouped according to the different needs of specific customers (for example, overseas visitors, corporate clients or government employees).**	Definite customer loyalty. Good reputation for personal service. Quick response to customer needs. 	Can be time-consuming dealing with consumer enquiries and complaints. Heavy focus on specific customers leaves business vulnerable if customer goes elsewhere. Extra staff training needed. Duplication of staff and resources.

DON'T FORGET

Although the same point can be made under more than one heading when grouping activities, you are unlikely to get the mark twice if you repeat the point in a Higher question. If you are asked to give the advantages and disadvantages of more than one type of grouping, make sure that you give **different answers for each**.

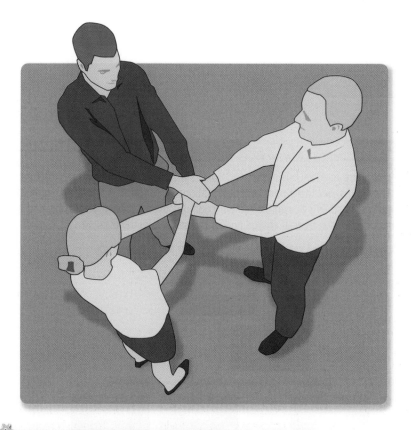

DON'T FORGET

In the exam, you may be asked to:
● **describe** the advantages and disadvantages of grouping activities
● **distinguish** between different types of grouping
or
● **describe** a particular type of grouping.

LET'S THINK ABOUT THIS

In some businesses, activities are grouped by what are deemed as **core activities**, or the main purpose of the business. These are then carried out by **line staff** who are directly involved with the product or service. **Support activities** are carried out by the functional departments discussed on page 43. These **support staff** help with the operations of the business. For example, in a college, the line staff are the lecturers, and the support staff are found in the HR, finance and admin sections.

In a large NHS hospital, who would be considered line and support staff?

FORMS OF ORGANISATIONAL STRUCTURE

ORGANISATION CHARTS

DON'T FORGET

Organisation charts also show the **chains of command** and the lines of communication. The longer the chain of command, the more difficult it will be for decisions to be made and for communication to travel up and down the organisation.

Organisation charts are used by businesses to inform staff and customers of the structure of the organisation. They will show the names and designations of staff and will clearly highlight lines of authority and responsibility. Sometimes colour-coding is used to identify sections, and there may be pictures of who is in overall charge and of the section leaders.

The chart below is a simplified version of a hierarchy in a secondary school.

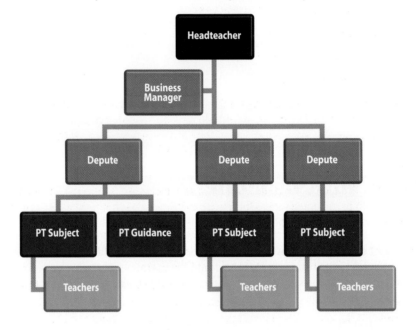

DON'T FORGET

An organisation chart also shows the **span of control**. This is the number of people who work under one manager.

Organisational relationships

Staff who share lateral relationships (are on the same level) are the same colour in this chart. Line relationships are vertical, so decisions and communication will travel from the headteacher down to the teachers and up again. The business manager has a staff relationship with the teaching staff, as he/she has no line authority but performs a specialist function within the school, where he/she will need to arrange staff cover for absent colleagues.

DIFFERENT TYPES OF STRUCTURE

Organisations can be structured in different ways. The most common is a **hierarchical structure**. The taller the structure, the more levels of management there are. This means that the span of control will be narrow, and there will be a long chain of command. Narrow spans of control tend to mean:

- a manageable group of workers to supervise
- smaller teams, so fewer people to do the work
- slower processes of communication
- decisions and information are passed down, information is passed up
- more tasks to be completed.

contd

DIFFERENT TYPES OF STRUCTURE contd

In general, there has been a shift towards organisations being 'flatter'. A flat organisation has fewer levels of management, wider spans of control and shorter chains of command. It also has fewer promotion opportunities. Wider spans of control tend to mean:

- greater need for delegation of duties
- more people requiring attention from one manager
- more empowerment to staff and less control by the manager
- information passed between staff more easily.

Other structures include the following:

Matrix – this type of structure tends to be used to manage projects. Teams consist of staff from different functional departments (effectively criss-crossing the organisation). This allows for the development of specialist skills and gives staff the opportunity to be more creative. There are team leaders, but no hierarchy, and all members will have the same level of authority and responsibility.

Entrepreneurial – this type of structure is used in small businesses. Decisions are made by a few people central to the organisation. This means that there does not need to be a lot of consultation, and decisions can be made quickly.

Centralised – this type of structure is often hierarchical, with top management taking decisions for the whole organisation. It is easier to standardise procedures.

Decentralised – these structures are more likely to delegate control and decision-making to sections and departments. This allows the organisation to be more responsive to changes in the market and local conditions. Staff members are empowered and will be more motivated, as they have more control.

DON'T FORGET

When answering questions on organisational charts and structures, make sure you use the correct terminology (**types of relationship, span of control, chain of command** ...).

 The following site gives more information on organisational structures: www.exampleoforganizationalchart.com/matrix.php

LET'S THINK ABOUT THIS

BIC is a very large manufacturer of razors, lighters and pens. It has simplified its operations to run from huge 'super-factories' that serve vast geographical markets. Product distribution is then organised by continent, with country managers reporting to their continental manager.

The organisation has a **matrix structure** based on two main lines of communication:
1) by **product category**, and
2) by **geographical region**. The matrix structure allows strong product expertise to be combined with strong operational structures in the geographic areas.

Describe the benefits to be gained in using a matrix structure.

ASPECTS OF ORGANISATIONAL STRUCTURE

DON'T FORGET

Restructuring on a regular basis is not recommended, as it will destabilise the organisation, create fear and uncertainty among staff and confuse customers.

Managers must make sure that they encourage the correct type of structure for their organisation. In order to do this, they must make staff aware of the chart and where they 'sit' within the structure. However, as well as this formalised approach, they should be prepared for the informal structures and relationships that can also develop.

FACTORS AFFECTING FORMAL STRUCTURES

1   **Size**. The larger the organisation, the greater the need for a formal structure as a method of control.

2   **Number of products/services**. The greater the number, the more need for a formal structure.

3   **Qualifications and skills of staff**. The more authority staff can be given, the flatter the structure can become.

4   **Marketplace**. Small, local markets or worldwide. The larger the marketplace, the greater the requirement for a formal structure.

DON'T FORGET

Informal communication in organisations is often referred to as the 'grapevine'.

Informal structures occur when staff members develop relationships outside their sections. This may happen because they are trying to get around 'red tape', or simply trying to get the job done efficiently.

CHANGING STRUCTURES

In recent years, organisations have had to alter their structures to meet the changing needs of business. **Restructuring**, **reorganising** and **realigning** are all terms that many of us are now familiar with. These changes often involve cutbacks in both resources and staff. Methods used include:

De-layering

This involves taking out a layer of management – usually middle managers – and increasing the span of control and responsibility of those left. By doing this, decisions can be taken more quickly, communications can be improved, salary bills cut and other resources saved.

Downsizing

DON'T FORGET

Make sure you can **explain** the term 'empowerment'. You will need to give the meaning and then state both the benefits and drawbacks to the organisation.

This means making the organisation smaller. In order to do this, parts of the business will be closed down and other parts merged. The business will lose valuable staff, and morale will drop. However, the aims of cutting costs and becoming more efficient should be achieved. In addition, certain aspects of the business could also be outsourced (see page 21), saving more money.

CORPORATE CULTURE

The corporate culture reflects the structure of a business – the more hierarchical the structure, the more formal the culture. The culture is made up of the business environment, the values of the business, its aims and its vision. Businesses will try to give a flavour of their culture in their mission statement. Corporate culture is built on with the use of logos, symbols, colour schemes, uniforms and advertising jingles.

Staff can be made aware of the culture in a variety of ways; for example, through social events, newsletters, competitions or training. It is believed that a strong corporate culture will pay dividends in:

- increased staff loyalty
- increased motivation and morale
- increased productivity
- better customer and employee relations
- better business image, which attracts new employees.

DON'T FORGET

Organisation charts go out of date very quickly as people leave and join the organisation.

Marks and Spencer is an organisation with a strong corporate identity in the UK. It has a well-known brand name and established retailing principles and uses well-known celebrities to endorse some of its products. Marks and Spencer has invested heavily in a state-of-the-art management system which has fostered a strong culture and staff loyalty. However, even with its successes, the company has continually had to develop and refashion its image to survive.

LET'S THINK ABOUT THIS

The company easyJet prefers to encourage an informal company culture with a very flat management structure. This eliminates the different layers of management that can make communication difficult. All office-based employees are encouraged to dress casually, and ties are actually banned – except for pilots. Flexible working practices are encouraged – remote working and 'hot desking' are part of the norm.

Using the internet, investigate other organisations that have strong corporate cultures.

3 BUSINESS DECISION AREAS: MARKETING AND OPERATIONS

MARKETING

THE ROLE AND IMPORTANCE OF MARKETING

Marketing is the process of finding out what consumers want and delivering it to them. It is sometimes defined as identifying, anticipating and satisfying the consumer. Usually, the main objective is to make a profit. However, if the business is in the public or voluntary sector, then the objective may be to increase public use of facilities, raise awareness of issues or promote campaigns.

There are three strands to marketing:

1 Marketing analysis – takes into consideration target markets, market segmentation and marketing strategy.

2 Marketing mix – looks at the product, price, place and promotion (the four Ps).

3 Market research – involves collecting information through analysis and testing.

DON'T FORGET

A business attitude to marketing can be either **product-orientated** (when the business concentrates on the production process and strives to make superior products) or **market-orientated** (when the business looks at what the customer wants and strives to provide it).

DON'T FORGET

Marketing is not just advertising and is not just about selling.

 There are lots of good marketing case studies available on the internet. Have a look at this one:
www.thetimes100.co.uk/case-study--using-marketing-mix-fashion-industry--135-327-1.php

EXTERNAL FACTORS

There are various factors that can affect the way in which goods and services are marketed. These are known as external factors, because they are outside the organisation. It is essential that the marketing department is aware of these factors and that campaigns are designed accordingly.

Political	There may be legislation that influences how products are perceived (for example, cigarettes and smoking).
Economic climate	In boom times, people will have more disposable income and will therefore be more receptive to marketing campaigns.
Social and fashion trends	Lifestyle dictates that we follow fashions, and marketing must be aware of the latest trends.
Technology	Advances in technology mean that some products have a very short life span.
Environment	Being aware of sustainable products and the effect of some products on the environment can be vital to success.
Competition	The world is now a much smaller place because of the internet; fierce competition can influence how an organisation operates.

DON'T FORGET

A **consumer market** is a market in which consumers purchase goods from retailers for personal use. An **industrial market** is a market in which groups of similar organisations purchase goods or services from other organisations. For example, some companies buy goods from other companies to sell.

LET'S THINK ABOUT THIS

This article gives an example of an industrial market.

Macsween seals Morrison's haggis deal

Haggis maker Macsween has landed a contract to supply the traditional Scottish product year-round to 100 Morrisons supermarkets south of the Border. The Edinburgh-based butcher said it expects overall sales to the English market to grow by about 60 per cent as a result of the deal.

James Macsween, director of the family-run firm, said the increase in demand in England and Wales was driven by the product becoming a popular ingredient in restaurant dishes such as haggis-stuffed mushrooms … The firm has just launched a single-portion haggis for people wanting to eat it alone or planning to use a small amount in a recipe.

Business Scotsman, 11 April 2009

DON'T FORGET

In the exam, you will often be asked to give the advantages and disadvantages of different types of marketing strategies.

THE MARKETING CONCEPT

Some key objectives of marketing are: to increase market share, to become a market leader and to increase the product portfolio. This means that marketing is a strategic activity. Marketing will help different types of business organisations to meet their strategic objectives. For example:

- A city council may launch a marketing campaign to publicise new bus and tram routes and stimulate an increase in the use of public transport.

- A private health club might want to attract more members by promoting its facilities.

- A college could attract more students by publicising its success rates and the opportunities that it offers to overseas students.

You will find lots of helpful notes on marketing here:
www.bized.co.uk/learn/business/marketing/analysis/index.htm

MARKET SHARE

Market share can be measured **either** by the number of products sold by all the different companies in the market who make the same or similar products, **or** by the value of the sales that each company has made. Pie charts are a good way of displaying this type of information.

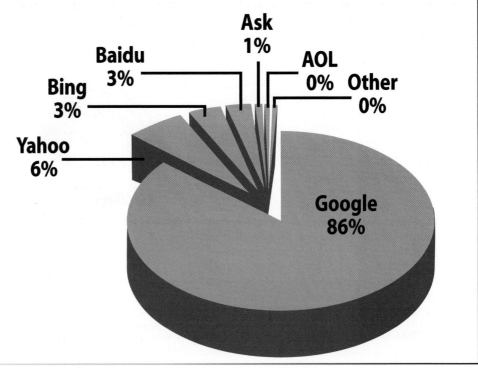

MARKET GROWTH

Market growth occurs when the number of people using a product increases. Some companies can increase their market share at the expense of others, or, if the whole market has grown sufficiently, then everyone will benefit from market growth.

MARKET SEGMENTATION

Market segmentation is the name given to the process of dividing up a market into different groups of consumers. The groups can be divided by:

- age
- gender
- religion
- income
- geographical location
- socio-economic group
- occupation
- family structure
- lifestyle.

Marketing and advertising can then be targeted to the appropriate group. For example, holidays to the Maldives and Seychelles will be advertised in newspapers like *The Times* and targeted at people of a certain age and income.

DON'T FORGET

The marketing and advertising industries grade people into the following classes based on their occupation and income: **A** = senior managers, professionals; **B** = middle managers; **C1** = non-manual workers, owners of small businesses; **C2** = skilled manual workers; **D** = semi-skilled and unskilled workers; **E** = those on benefits, casual labourers and pensioners.

NICHE MARKETING

A niche market is an even smaller part of the market. It is a section within a market segment. A niche market is made up of people who are prepared to pay more either for exclusivity, or because they have to – for example, people with special dietary needs (see the article below). Niche markets that are profitable will attract competition, but they do have a high risk of failure if consumers cease to be attracted to the product.

 LET'S THINK ABOUT THIS

Read this article. Can you identify other products that might appeal to niche markets?

Gluten-free bread sales are on a roll

A special gluten and wheat-free bread created by an Edinburgh mum is proving to be a bestseller. Lucinda Bruce-Gardyne developed the Genius loaf after struggling to find snacks that her seven-year-old son Robin could stomach. The youngster suffers painful reactions to gluten. The mother of three, who previously cooked at a Michelin-star restaurant, spent three years working on the bread.

The loaf is now the best-selling product in Tesco's 'free from' range. There are about 600,000 people in Britain, including 80,000 children, who are unable to eat gluten.

Edinburgh Evening News, 23 May 2009

DON'T FORGET

Make sure you can explain the difference between **differentiated marketing** and **undifferentiated marketing**. Differentiated marketing is when a company aims different products at different market segments (for example, a car manufacturer which has different types of car for low- and high-income groups). **Undifferentiated marketing** is when one product is aimed at the majority of the population (for example, Andrex toilet paper).

3 BUSINESS DECISION AREAS:
MARKETING AND OPERATIONS
THE MARKETING MIX

The best method to market a new product is to look at the four Ps. These are:

Product   **Price**   **Place**   **Promotion**

1   The **product** (including the image, brand and after-sales service) must be what consumers want. It must be suitable for a particular purpose.

2   The **price** must be at a level that consumers are prepared to pay, yet must still make a profit for the company.

3   The product must be sold in the correct **place**, whether through wholesalers, retailers, agents, importers/exporters, online or through catalogues.

4   The product needs to be **promoted** to the correct target market. The marketing mix of these **four Ps** must be right to ensure success.

PRODUCT DEVELOPMENT AND LIFE CYCLE

Before a product can be launched onto the market, it must pass through various stages. The idea needs to be analysed, finance made available, a prototype used to test market reaction and then further modification made before production.

If this is successful, then a new product will go through five stages in its life cycle. These are:

1   **Introduction**. The product is launched onto the market.

2   **Growth**. Sales increase as consumers become familiar with the product, and competitors enter the market.

3   **Maturity**. Growth slows, and increased competition means that lower prices must be introduced.

4   **Saturation**. Consumer tastes change, and sales fall.

5   **Decline**. There is little demand for the product, and it is withdrawn from the market.

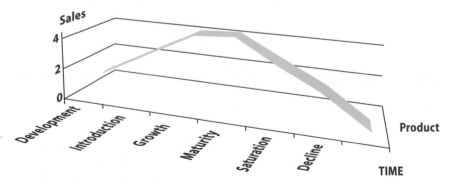

The length of the life cycle depends on the product. Certain products naturally have a longer life than others – fashions only last a season, but some products, like HP Sauce®, have been around

contd

PRODUCT DEVELOPMENT AND LIFE CYCLE contd

for years (as have Kellogg's Corn Flakes® and Fairy Liquid®). This is because these products have strong brands and have used extension strategies to prevent them from going into decline. HP Sauce® is available in a range of formats and sizes, from the famous glass bottle to the squeezable plastic bottle. There are also other products in the range, including a reduced-salt-and-sugar version of the original sauce that was released in 2008.

Most businesses will develop product lines to remain profitable. This means that they are able to spread the risk if one of their products fails or suffers bad publicity. It also allows the company to try out new products on loyal consumers. The company can become specialist producers and increase their market share.

DON'T FORGET

The product mix, or portfolio, is the range of goods that a company produces under one brand name. This helps to spread the risk when some products are in decline.

EXTENSION STRATEGIES

Extension strategies aim to stop products from going into decline, and include:

- changing the packaging to make it appeal to different consumers
- improving the product (cleaning products are often marketed as 'new and improved')
- rebranding the product and changing the name
- changing the price
- selling in a different way (for example, from a home catalogue or online)
- developing new markets.

BRANDING

Brands allow the products and services of one company to be differentiated from those of its competitors – a brand usually has an established name and logo that make the consumer aware of the product, its value and its quality. A brand's image is generated as a result of consumer perception of what the product does.

When a successful name is used to launch a new product or to modify a product, this is known as brand extension. For example, Apple has used its name to move away from computers and into the new markets of MP3 players (with the iPod®) and mobile phones (with the iPhone®).

Advantages of branding	Disadvantages of branding
Establishes consumer loyalty.	Can take time to establish a brand name.
Product is instantly recognisable – higher prices can be charged.	Can be more expensive – advertising and packaging cost more.
Easier to launch a new product and make changes.	Open to increased competition and fakes.
A brand is an asset on a balance sheet.	One incident of bad publicity could cause failure.
A product can come to be known by a brand name (for example, a hoover).	
Consumers will buy brands endorsed by celebrities.	

LET'S THINK ABOUT THIS

Large stores and supermarkets often have their own product labels, known as **own brands**. These tend to be relatively cheap and can sometimes be perceived as inferior. However, some supermarkets have also launched their own 'luxury' ranges, so that they can compete with branded products (for example, Asda's 'Extra special' range). Check out this website for a case study on own brands and their advantages and disadvantages: http://tutor2u.net/business/marketing/casestudy_supermarket_ownlabel.asp

3 BUSINESS DECISION AREAS: MARKETING AND OPERATIONS

PRICE, PLACE AND PROMOTION

PRICE

Charging the right price is a very important part of the marketing mix. The price will depend on a number of factors, including:

- where the product is in its life cycle (at a point of growth or maturity)
- what price competitors are charging
- expected profit
- what the customer is willing to pay
- government regulations
- the targeted market segment
- the economic climate
- how much promotion and advertising is needed
- the time of year (if it is a seasonal product).

Some short-term pricing strategies include:

Demand pricing	Prices vary with the product (for example, the cost of tea may rise when the harvest is poor).
Value/ Premium pricing	Due to consumer perceptions of the item, higher prices can be charged (for example, sports cars).
Psychological pricing	Charging £19.89 instead of £20.00.
Skimming	High prices are charged for new products because they face little competition and still have novelty value (for example, expensive games consoles). Once the market segment is saturated, the price falls.
Penetration pricing	Used when an organisation wants to enter a market. They will charge a price much lower than the competitors until their product becomes popular – then they will raise the price again.
Destroyer pricing	Prices are set at a low level, often running at a loss in the short term. This is used to eliminate competition and force others to leave the market.
Promotional pricing	Sales are boosted by lowering prices for a short period of time.
Discriminatory pricing	Different prices are charged for the same item depending on the time of day or year (for example, seats on aircraft).
Loss leaders	Consumers are tempted into a store to buy something at a low and unprofitable price. It is hoped that, once the consumer is in the store, they will buy other products at normal prices.

DON'T FORGET

Businesses may also use **long-term pricing strategies** for different types of markets and conditions. **High pricing** is used when the business wants to offer high-quality products. **Low pricing** is used when the business charges less than its competitors, in order to attract consumers. This is usually when the demand for a product is very sensitive to price (for example, DVDs). **Competitive pricing** is when the price is set in line with what competitors are charging.

DON'T FORGET

An increasing number of sales are made online, effectively cutting out the 'middleman'.

PLACE

Place describes **how** the product gets to the consumer or market. Place often depends on the product itself. The route that it takes is called the **channel of distribution**:

Manufacturer > Wholesaler > Retailer > Consumer

PROMOTION

Promotion is used to make consumers aware of products and services and to persuade them that they want the product or service. It is also used to inform consumers about the product and to remind them of the benefits of buying it. Promotion can come in a variety of forms, for example:

You can see from the diagram that advertising is only one part of promotion. Product placement is the term used when a firm pays for its product to appear within a film or DVD (for example, the Sony laptop that appears in the film *Casino Royale*). Product endorsement is the term used when a celebrity is paid to wear or use a product. For example, Tiger Woods, Gary Lineker, Andy Murray, Nicole Kidman, Justin Timberlake and Cheryl Cole have all boosted product sales.

Into- and out-of-the-pipeline promotions

Other forms of promotion can be divided as follows:

Into-the-pipeline promotions (offered by manufacturers to retailers)	Out-of-the-pipeline promotions (offered by retailers to consumers)
Buy goods on a sale-or-return basis.	BOGOFs = Buy one, get one free.
Special credit terms.	Free samples handed out at demonstrations or in-store tastings.
Bonuses for sales made.	Coupons and vouchers connected to free offers.
Running competitions and displays at checkouts.	Competitions (usually free entry when you buy the product).
Dealer loaders ('3 for the price of 2', or 'Buy one case and get half a case free').	A percentage of the product free ('20% extra in this pack!').

DON'T FORGET

Advertising can be conducted through a variety of different media. The channel used will depend on the product and target market. Some examples of advertising channels include TV, radio, cinema, magazines, newspapers, outdoor billboards, bus shelters, mailshots and the internet.

LET'S THINK ABOUT THIS

The singer Duffy endorsed Diet Coke® and was seen in an advert riding a bicycle through a supermarket. There were 22 complaints to the **Advertising Standards Authority** – the body that makes sure that all advertising, wherever it appears, meets the standards laid down in the advertising codes. Look on their website for further information: www.asa.org.uk

You can view the advert and details about the complaints here: www.guardian.co.uk/media/2009/jun/17/duffy-diet-coke-bicycle-ad

Can you find any other adverts that have received complaints?

3 BUSINESS DECISION AREAS: MARKETING AND OPERATIONS

SELLING AND SALES PROMOTION

There are a variety of ways to sell a product to the customer. These include:

- Mail order – selling through catalogues.
- Direct mail – often seen as 'junk' mail, but usually reaches correct target market.
- Personal selling – people who sell door-to-door, often double glazing or driveway paving.
- Internet selling – this is the biggest growth area, as nearly anything can be bought online.
- Newspapers and magazines – by completing coupons or telephoning direct.

MARKET RESEARCH

All businesses need to gather information about their target markets, consumer tastes, current trends and how their products are performing. This information needs to be analysed correctly and be reliable (see pages 26–27). There are two main types of market research:

1 **Desk research** – this is a cheap way to gather data using secondary sources of information. The drawback is that it uses historical data that may have been collected for other purposes.

2 **Field research** – this is primary data collected in person, generally in the form of a questionnaire or survey. It is usually up to date and has been collected for the correct purpose.

Different methods of field research include:

- telephone survey
- postal survey
- observation
- hall test (asking customers to try a product and give feedback)
- EPOS (electronic point of sale)
- personal interview
- consumer/focus groups
- test-marketing a product in one area only
- consumer audit (used when a lot of data is required; tends to be ongoing research).

When testing the market for research purposes, it is not always possible to survey everyone. In this case, a **sample** is taken to try to gauge consumer reactions. There are three different forms of sampling:

contd

DON'T FORGET

Always remember to expand on bullet points. Take note of the keyword in the question – does it ask you to **describe**, **explain** or **discuss**? Answer appropriately and note how many marks are allocated to the question.

DON'T FORGET

There are four main types of advertising:
1 **Informative advertising** – often used by the government (for example, what to do if you think you have swineflu).
2 **Persuasive advertising** – used by manufacturers to get consumers to buy their products.
3 **Corporate advertising** – used to sell the whole company (for example, slogans).
4 **Generic advertising** – when a number of manufacturers come together to advertise their products (for example, encouraging consumers to buy more milk).

MARKET RESEARCH contd

Random	Quota	Stratified random
People are selected at random from either the telephone directory or other available lists. They must be interviewed even if not contactable on the first occasion. This can be an expensive system to operate. 	Set criteria will be allocated to researchers, and they must interview people according to these criteria (for example, 20 males under 16 years of age; 40 married people aged 35).	This is when the random sample is split according to socio-economic groups. The sample taken must reflect the overall grouping (for example, if 10 per cent of the population is in group C1, then the sample must reflect this). 

DON'T FORGET

You need to know the advantages and disadvantages of the different methods of field research. You should also be able to suggest when to use each one.

PUBLIC RELATIONS

A public-relations department is responsible for the image of an organisation. It communicates with external bodies such as the press, the media, the government, shareholders and all consumers. As its main role is to portray a positive image at all times, the PR department will prepare press releases, facilitate donations to charity, sponsor events on behalf of the organisation, encourage product endorsement and hold press conferences.

 Check out the following link to find out about changing the packaging of cereal boxes: www.tutor2u.net/blog/index.php/business-studies/comments/snap-crackle-and-crumbs-are-cereal-boxes-toast-now/

DON'T FORGET

Packaging is sometimes referred to as the **fifth P** (see page 54). The packaging of a product is extremely important, and the size, weight, shape, design and colour of the product should be taken into consideration. It is also important to consider the cost of packaging and its impact on the environment.

 ## LET'S THINK ABOUT THIS

PR is a very important part of marketing. Over the years, there have been some famous PR blunders that have caused a lot of damage to the products and companies involved – for example, the chaotic scenes in 2008 at the opening of the new Terminal 5 at Heathrow Airport, or the chief executive of Barclaycard® suggesting that clever consumers should avoid credit cards.

To find out more about these and other PR disasters, access the following:

www.telegraph.co.uk/finance/newsbysector/transport/3047854/Terminal-5-joins-the-list-of-top-PR-blunders.html

OPERATIONS

THE ROLE OF OPERATIONS

The role of operations is to produce goods and/or services, so that the organisation has something to sell. This should enable it to reach its objectives, make a profit and generate wealth.

DECISION AREAS FOR OPERATIONS MANAGERS

Purchasing	● Deciding what stock to buy. ● Selecting a supplier. ● Reorder levels (how much/how often to reorder?).
System design	● Factory layout. ● Production processes. ● Workflow between production areas. ● Staffing (who? how many? when?). ● Automation (use of machinery and/or robots).
System operation	● Stock control. ● Quantity of stock to hold (depending on space, cost, turnover). ● Storage areas (how much, and where?). ● Conditions required for holding stock. ● How to minimise risk to stock (for example, premature deterioration or theft).

THE PRODUCTION CYCLE

The production of goods and services has three distinct stages – each of which must be carried out successfully to ensure consistent quality and to maximise profits.

| Input (raw materials and labour) | Process (steps taken to produce the goods/service) | Output (the finished product ready for warehousing and distribution) |

The processing part of operations is sometimes referred to as the **production cycle** – the time it takes for the goods or services to be prepared for distribution to the customer.

PAYMENT SYSTEMS

Different companies use different payment systems for staff. Some companies will use different systems for different types of employees. For example, managers and office staff may be paid a flat rate, while manual workers may be paid an hourly rate with overtime. You should know how the different systems work.

Flat rate: Set salary per annum divided into 12 monthly payments. Doesn't reward staff for increased high level of effort but allows them a guaranteed monthly income.

Time rate: Paid per hour (e.g. £15 per hour). Simple to calculate. Pays for actual time spent at work and not for output.

Piece rate: Paid an agreed rate for the amount of work done. Payment by results – sometimes sacrificing quality for quantity.

Overtime: Normally an hourly rate plus an increase for extra hours worked (double time). Acts as an incentive to work more than the contracted hours.

Commission: Reward for the amount of product or service sold to customer – usually paid on top of basic salary. Paid as a percentage of the product's sale value.

Annualised hours: Paid assuming a basic working week of 37.5 hours. Same amount received each week/month. Depending on demand, may have to work more or less some months.

Bonus: Given as a reward for hard work – varies according to time and economic conditions.

Fringe benefits: Extras that do not appear on the payslip – may include private health care, subsidised canteens, company pension schemes.

Profit-sharing: Workers may use part of salary to buy shares in the company.

 **DON'T FORGET**

You might be asked to **compare** payment systems, so make sure you know the similarities and differences between them.

Would you work for free? BA hopes so!
http://news.bbc.co.uk/1/hi/business/8102862.stm

 LET'S THINK ABOUT THIS

In 2009, there was a huge row over MPs' expenses. To see what kind of expenses were being claimed, have a look at these websites:

www.telegraph.co.uk/news/newstopics/mps-expenses/5310200/MPs-expenses-Paying-bills-for-Tory-grandees.html

http://news.bbc.co.uk/1/hi/uk_politics/8039273.stm

Select at least three examples of MPs' expense claims. Do you think any of them can be justified?

STOCK CONTROL

Efficient stock control helps ensure that customer orders can be met in a cost-effective way.

Good stock management means getting the balance right – you don't want to hold too much or too little stock. Holding the wrong amount of stock can create a number of problems for a company.

Too much stock

- High storage, maintenance, security, insurance, lighting and handling costs.
- Takes up space that could be used for something else.
- Money tied up in stock could have been used for something else.
- Possibility of holding unsold stock.
- Stock could get damaged or deteriorate with age.
- Stock could go out of fashion or become obsolete.
- The longer stock is stored, the higher the chance of theft.

Too little stock

Although holding minimum stock can help avoid many of the problems listed above, there are still pitfalls:

- Difficult to cope with changes in demand.
- Late deliveries of materials may result in inability to meet orders, or a halt in production.
- More difficult to cope with shortages in materials.
- May have to order more often, which means higher administration costs.
- Reputation may suffer if orders are not met.

DON'T FORGET

Effective stock control is about deciding **what**, **when** and **how much** to order:

- maximum stock level – depends on storage space, security, cost, finance
- minimum stock level – taking into account ordering and delivery times
- reorder level – depends on average daily usage and lead time (time it takes for new supplies to arrive)
- reorder quantity – the amount that will be needed to restore stock to maximum level

JIT STOCK CONTROL

Advantages	Disadvantages
Money not tied up in stock.	High dependence on suppliers (late delivery could affect production/sales).
Less space needed.	
Close relationship built with suppliers.	May lose discounts for bulk buying.
Less wastage due to deterioration.	Cannot cope with unexpected changes in demand.
Less wastage due to fashion changes.	Higher transport costs for more frequent deliveries.
Costs reduced.	Higher admin costs.
	Unexpected losses of stock (theft, fire and so on) could affect production/sales.

Read the article on stock management at:
http://tutor2u.net/business/production/stock-management-other-aspects.htm

CENTRALISED STOCK-CONTROL SYSTEMS

Advantages	Disadvantages
Improved security (easier to ensure doors are locked; could use security staff).	Getting stock to relevant departments can be time-consuming.
Reduced costs (bulk purchases = economies of scale).	More stock can mean more wastage.
Fewer and smaller purchases mean lower transport/delivery costs.	Harder to meet specialised requirements of departments.
Reduces duplication of stock held by company.	Central stock may be remote from production, wasting time moving materials.
Specialist staff control ordering, issuing and purchasing.	Cost implications of moving stock from remote store.
Agreed procedures set up for whole organisation.	

Is the government good at stock management – or just lucky?
www.healthy.net/scr/news.asp?Id=10121

LET'S THINK ABOUT THIS

JIT can be risky, but so can over-stocking. Read the article at:
http://news.bbc.co.uk/1/hi/business/696695.stm.

What went wrong, and what were the consequences?

DON'T FORGET

JIT = just in time. Stock arrives in time to be used in production, and goods are not produced unless orders have been taken. Successful JIT depends on reliable suppliers, good quality-control procedures and a supply of skilled workers.

STOCK LEVELS AND SUPPLIERS

FACTORS TO CONSIDER WHEN SETTING STOCK REORDER LEVELS

DON'T FORGET

In **computerised stock control**, a database is used to record stock. Reordering is done automatically when the reorder level has been met (for example, in supermarkets). One advantage is that bestsellers and 'slow movers' can be easily identified. The main disadvantages are set-up and running costs.

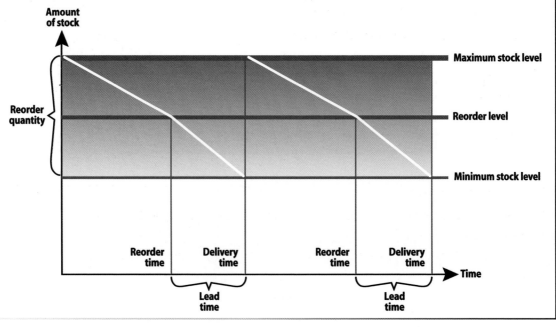

 Read this article to see how the NHS puts sustainability into its purchasing mix.
www.ethicalperformance.com/europeamericas/articleView.php?articleID=3865

CHOOSING A SUPPLIER

Good suppliers are invaluable. Finding a supplier that you can rely on to provide good-quality stock when you require it can help to ensure that your own business runs smoothly. When choosing a supplier, you need to consider:

Quality

- Can the supplier supply the quality of materials needed?
- Can the supplier supply a consistent quality?

Quantity

- Can the supplier deliver the quantities required?

DON'T FORGET

Choosing a supplier is a balancing act between cost and quality/service. The factors taken into consideration when choosing a supplier are often referred to as the **purchasing mix**.

Timing

- Can the supplier meet the required delivery dates?
- Is the supplier likely to deliver on time?

Price

- Is the price acceptable?
- Are discounts offered?
- Are credit terms available?
- Are there charges for delivery or insurance?

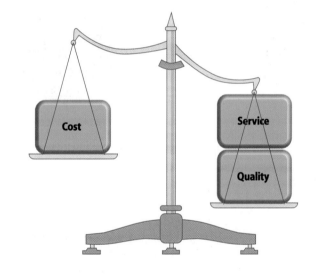

Dependability

- Is the supplier likely to remain in business?
- Is the supplier respectable/honest/trustworthy?
- Does the supplier have reliable delivery systems?
- Can you get references from companies that currently use them?

LET'S THINK ABOUT THIS

'The ultimate goal of a purchasing policy is to control costs. But good supplier relationships are based on more than just money.'

Read the rest of this article at: www.businesslink.gov.uk/bdotg/action/detail?type=CASE%20STUDIES&itemId=1075059490

You should also take a look at www.bizymoms.com/entrepreneur/library/supplier002.html

What other factors are identified in these sources? What are the characteristics of a poor supplier, and what are the potential consequences to an organisation?

3 BUSINESS DECISION AREAS: MARKETING AND OPERATIONS

TYPES OF PRODUCTION

The choice of production method depends on the product, the size of the market and the size of the business, as well as the finance and technology available. You should be able to describe the three types of production.

BATCH PRODUCTION

This type of production is used in bakeries and to produce paint, sports shoes, wallpaper and so on.

- Groups of similar products are made at the same time.
- The whole batch completes each stage in the process before passing to the next.
- Raw materials can be bought in bulk, reducing costs.
- As staff members become experts in their part of the process, productivity increases.
- As staff members become more experienced, quality increases.

FLOW PRODUCTION

This type of production is used on a car production line.

- Items move along an assembly line.
- Each step in the process leads to completion of the final product.
- Machinery is used to reduce labour costs.
- Large quantities can be produced.
- The cost of individual products can be reduced.
- High use of automation and CAM means that products can be produced around the clock.
- There is little or no variation in the items produced.

> **DON'T FORGET**
>
> Flow production is also called **mass production**.

JOB PRODUCTION

This type of production is used to produce custom-built furniture, tailored suits and wedding dresses.

- A single product is made to customer specifications.
- Skilled workers make the product.
- Used for production of one-off items.
- Higher prices can be charged.
- Can be motivational to workers.
- High quality.

For more information on different methods of production, see the following websites: http://tutor2u.net/business/gcse/production_flow.htm
http://tutor2u.net/business/gcse/production_job.htm
http://tutor2u.net/business/gcse/production_batch.htm

LABOUR-INTENSIVE AND CAPITAL-INTENSIVE PRODUCTION

In the developing world, production methods are usually labour-intensive. In the developed world, many companies use automated production methods (capital-intensive production). Most manufacturing companies use a mix of both labour- and capital-intensive methods.

Labour-intensive production requires a relatively high number of workers compared to capital-intensive production. It is used when:

- the labour supply is cheap and readily available
- the product requires craftsmanship or special expertise
- the business is small
- there is no finance for expensive machinery.

The disadvantages of labour-intensive production are:

- a skilled workforce can be expensive to pay and train
- only small-scale production may be possible
- it cannot take advantage of economies of scale
- it is difficult to replace ill or absent staff
- the quality of products has to be closely monitored for consistency.

Capital-intensive production requires heavy investment in machinery, equipment and vehicles, rather than in people and labour. It is used when:

- a standard product is being produced
- standard operations can be used
- labour is scarce or expensive
- consistency of the product and its quality are required
- economies of scale are desirable
- continuous production is required.

The disadvantages of capital-intensive production are:

- it is expensive to set up
- breakdowns can be costly in terms of lost production
- individual customer requirements cannot be met
- worker motivation can be low due to the repetitive work.

DON'T FORGET

The two main methods of measuring the efficiency of production are known as **method study** and **work measurement**. Method study looks at how a job is being done with a view to improving it.

S Select the task to be analysed.
R Record how it is done now.
E Examine the information collected.
D Develop a better method.
I Install the new method.
M Maintain the new method.

Work measurement establishes how long tasks should take, so that standard times can be identified for each task.

LET'S THINK ABOUT THIS

Have a look at these websites. What production and distribution methods are used by Irn Bru?

www.filter.ac.uk/database/getinsight.php?id=43&seq=11
www.agbarr.co.uk/

QUALITY

Producing a high-quality product is all about satisfying the needs of your customer. The aim is to provide a product or service that meets (or exceeds) the expectations of your customer, at a price they are prepared to pay.

Quality is important because it:

- gives competitive advantage
- encourages return purchases
- provides customers with information and builds consumer confidence in the brand
- reduces costs incurred in solving post-sale problems
- helps improve efficiency.

QUALITY INPUTS

To ensure that a product or service is produced to a high quality, an organisation must ensure that the raw materials used are of the right quality.

Quality inputs help ensure:

- that the manufacturer can make accurate claims on their own products (for example, 'sourced from sustainable forests', 'free from GM products', 'organically grown')
- less waste for the manufacturer (if the raw materials meet their criteria and they produce a high-quality product, there will be fewer customer complaints and returns)
- less down-time as a result of having to clean or repair equipment
- improved efficiency
- consistency of output (if you can rely on the quality of your inputs, you know what to expect as your output).

 **DON'T FORGET**

The supplier may be asked to provide evidence of their own quality procedures so that the manufacturer can trust the source.

 Many companies publish a statement on their quality procedures and standards on their website. Look up www.agbarr.co.uk/agbarr/newsite/ces_general.nsf/wpg/corporate_responsibility-quality_and_food_safety

QUALITY MANAGEMENT

Effective and consistent use of quality-management techniques helps ensure the production of a high-quality product or service. Organisations may use the following methods to help ensure good quality management:

Benchmarking – the business is compared to other similar organisations (quality and price of product, customer satisfaction). The business adopts the best methods identified through best practice in the industry.

Quality assurance – the product is checked at key points in the production process to ensure that it is of the required standard. Unacceptable products are discarded. Products could be scrutinised at any stage of the production process using spot checks.

Quality control – the product is checked at the end of the process to ensure that it is fit for purpose.

Quality circles – groups of workers (from managers to manual workers) meet to discuss the best methods and try to identify where improvements can be made.

Continuous improvement – encourages workers doing the job to make suggestions. The people who know the production process best are in a good position to see what works well and what does not.

TQM – the whole organisation is responsible for the management of quality, and awareness of quality is promoted throughout the company. The focus is on doing things right the first time and producing quality products every time without defects.

Staff – the whole organisation must be committed to quality. Through teamwork and training, staff members feel responsible for quality and know what is expected and how to achieve it. Staff are motivated to provide a quality product/service.

Standards – clearly-defined standards and policies are implemented to ensure quality at all times. BSI (British Standards Institution) awards are used to show that quality has been approved. Trade logos (such as the Red Lion mark on eggs, or quality-assurance stickers on meat) show that products have met industry standards. European standard awards show that European/international standards have been met.

British
Lion eggs

DON'T FORGET

Good quality = happy customers = repeat business = more profit.

Materials and equipment – good quality raw materials are used. Equipment is checked to ensure that it produces a product of the required quality. Appropriate methods are used to ensure product quality.

A summary of this topic can be found at: www.bized.co.uk/educators/16-19/business/production/presentation/qualcontrol.ppt
Information on international standards can be found at: www.iso.org/iso/theisocafe.htm

LET'S THINK ABOUT THIS

Visit the Trading Standards website and search 'product recall'. What products have been recalled recently? What tend to be the main reasons for product recall?

www.tradingstandards.gov.uk/

WAREHOUSING, DISTRIBUTION AND DELIVERY

WAREHOUSING

Warehousing is the storage of finished stock/goods. This can be **centralised** or **decentralised** depending on the company. The type of warehousing used depends on the type of stock being held, the finance available for storage, the company policy and the size, number and location of customers to be supplied.

Centralised warehousing

- All stock is held in one place before it is sent out.
- Stock control is easier to manage.
- Stock is easier to secure.
- Easier to maintain correct environment (temperature, humidity and so on).
- Might be a long way from warehouse to point of sale.

Decentralised warehousing

- Stock held in smaller quantities.
- Stock held in several locations.
- Stock closer to customer before being sent out.

DISTRIBUTION

The **distribution channel** describes how a product or service gets from the manufacturer to the customer. There are three main routes:

1 manufacturer → customer
2 manufacturer → retailer → customer
3 manufacturer → wholesaler → retailer → customer.

The chosen distribution route for a product is called the **distribution mix**. The distribution mix depends on:

- **the product** – specialist products (for example, hospital equipment) are often sold directly to the customer
- **legal restrictions** – for example, certain drugs are only available by prescription and must be sold through pharmacies
- **image** – is it an 'exclusive' product or something 'cheap and cheerful' for the mass market?
- **distribution capacity** – does the manufacturer have its own delivery fleet or sales staff?
- **finance** – how much does the manufacturer have available for distribution?
- **the reliability of other companies in the chain** – if the wholesaler/retailer is unreliable, it may be best to sell direct to the customer
- **consumer buying habits** – is the market used to buying from local retailers or online?
- **the market** – local, national or international.

In recent years, many factors have had an effect on distribution methods. Some of these are:

contd

DISTRIBUTION contd

- increased opening hours
- increased diversification (stores supplying food, clothes, gardening products, pet food, insurance – all under one roof)
- growth in retail parks and shopping centres
- increased call-centre sales (buying insurance online or by phone)
- decline of independent retailers
- need to reduce costs to remain competitive
- pursuit of profits
- own-brand products.

 Look up http://www.bbc.co.uk/schools/gcsebitesize/business/production/ locationanddistributionrev1.shtml

DON'T FORGET

Direct sales means selling directly to the customer. This is becoming increasingly popular as more people shop online.

DON'T FORGET

Branded retailing is when a retailer sells its own brand of goods.

DELIVERY

Most stock is delivered using road, rail, sea or air.

Road

- relatively quick and cheap if the distance is not too great; door-to-door delivery
- modern vehicles specially designed to transport specific goods (for example, refrigerated lorries); many organisations have their own delivery vehicles
- disadvantage = legal restrictions on the number of hours lorry-drivers can drive.

Rail

- specialist rail freight terminals, allowing distribution from main centres
- can be cheaper than roads if there is a lot to distribute; and safer than roads for some products
- more environmentally friendly than roads; reduces road congestion.

Sea

- mainly used for petrol products, minerals and coal in Scotland
- can be used to get goods to northern and western islands
- useful for importing/exporting bulky goods, but delivery times can be lengthy.

Air

- caters well for longer, international travel
- faster than other methods
- ideal for smaller electronic components.

DON'T FORGET

Delivery transport may be internally or externally sourced – an organisation might have its own delivery fleet (internal), or it might contract the work out to other organisations (external).

LET'S THINK ABOUT THIS

Environmental considerations are very important when distributing goods. Find out how ASDA is tackling this issue in its *2009 Global Sustainability Report* at: http://walmartstores.com/sites/sustainabilityreport/2009/en_logistics.html

When looking after the planet, we often hear about the importance of the three Rs (reduce, reuse, recycle) and sustainability. What does sustainability mean?

FINANCE

FINANCIAL MANAGEMENT

The finance section plays an important role in an organisation by providing information to managers that allows them to make strategic decisions, control costs and maximise profit. The finance section will:

Monitor business funds
- Pay the bills
- Maintain credit control

Provide information to management
- Prepare financial Statements
- Pay wages and salaries

Monitor internal financial information
- Monitor cash flows
- Monitor cash budgets

FINANCIAL RECORDS AND STATEMENTS

All organisations must keep financial records. The main financial statements are shown below.

The trading account

The trading account calculates the difference between the amount of goods sold by the firm and those brought in. It shows a profit or loss before any expenses.

The key terminology used in the trading account is:

PATTERSON ENTERPRISES
TRADING PROFIT AND LOSS ACCOUNT FOR THE YEAR ENDING 31 MARCH 2010

	£s	£s
Net sales (turnover)		150,000
Less cost of goods sold		
Opening stock	25,000	
+ purchases	62,000	
	87,000	
Less closing stock	34,000	
Cost of goods sold		53,000
GROSS PROFIT		£ 97,000

Net sales (turnover) the money brought in from selling a product, less any returns.

Opening stock the value of goods held by the business at the start of the financial year.

Purchases the cost of goods brought in by the organisation for resale.

Closing stock the value of goods held by the business at the end of the financial year.

Cost of goods sold the cost of the goods to the business.

Gross profit/loss the difference between the sales and purchases figures.

Profit and loss account

The **profit and loss account** shows the net profit (or loss) made by the organisation after all expenses have been subtracted from the gross profit.

PROFIT AND LOSS ACCOUNT

	£s	£s
Gross profit		97,000
Less expenses		
Rent and rates	12,370	
Heat and light	18,000	
Advertising	2,500	
Insurance	3,000	
Wages and salaries	36,630	
		72,500
Net profit		£24,500

DON'T FORGET

These documents are **historic**, as they show what has happened over a period of time. The balance sheet is only correct for the date for which it is prepared.

contd

FINANCIAL RECORDS AND STATEMENTS contd

The balance sheet

PATTERSON ENTERPRISES
BALANCE SHEET AS AT 31 MARCH 2010

	£000s	£000s	£000s
Fixed assets			
Buildings			1,250
Motor vehicles			425
Fixtures and fittings			185
			1,860
+ Current assets			
Stock		34	
Debtors		81	
Bank		45	
Cash		22	
		182	
– Current liabilities			
Creditors	76		
Taxation	50	126	
Net current assets (working capital)			56
Net assets employed			£1,916
Financed by			
Opening capital			£1,600
+ Net profit		£24.5	
- Drawings		14.5	10
			1,610
+ Bank loan			306
			£1,916

The **balance sheet** shows the value of the business at a set date. The **fixed assets** section shows the items that the business will hold for longer than one year. The **current assets** are items that can change on a daily basis. The **current liabilities** are monies that the business owes within the financial year/short term. The **financed by** section sets out how the business is financed.

DON'T FORGET

You need to know what the financial statements contain and be able to distinguish between different key terms.

OTHER KEY TERMS

Debtors – customers that owe the business money for goods sold on credit.

Creditors – suppliers of goods purchased on credit by the business and to whom the business owes money.

Net current assets/Working capital is the difference between the current assets and the current liabilities.

Opening capital is the amount invested by the owner in the business.

Drawings are any monies taken out of the business by the owner for personal use.

 This site gives access to many companies' annual reports:
www.orderannualreports.com/?cp_code=P241

LET'S THINK ABOUT THIS

What is the importance of the annual accounts, and how can they show that an organisation has met its objectives? Who will be interested in accessing the annual accounts, and why?

4 BUSINESS DECISION AREAS: FINANCE AND HUMAN RESOURCES

FINANCIAL INFORMATION

WHO WANTS TO USE FINANCIAL INFORMATION?

Shareholders

- Want to know how a company is performing and if they will get a good return on their investment.
- Want to compare performance with competitors and investigate any big differences.
- Are kept informed by the annual accounts as to the progress of the company and with indications as to whether they should buy or sell their shares.

Management

- Need to be able to find out if the business is performing, in order to set targets that will allow them to meet predictions and fulfil plans.
- Can use the accounts to compare how the firm has performed over a number of years.

Employees

- Will always be interested in the viability of the business and its ability to pay their salaries.
- Will want to monitor cash flow.

Customers

- May have ethical and environmental issues.
- May simply want to know if the company will continue to trade.

Competitors

- Will be interested in plans for expansion.
- Will want to know if the business has increased or decreased its market share.

Government

- Will want to know the future plans for the business.
- Will want to know how much it is making, in order to collect taxes.

Analysts

- Collate information and make comparisons with other businesses in the same industry or research sector, for research and statistical purposes.

Creditors/lenders

- Assess the viability of the business and whether it is in a good position to pay back any loans and meet its commitments.

DON'T FORGET

Make sure you know the difference between a **shareholder** and a **stakeholder**. Don't include competitors when talking about stakeholders in a business.

CHARACTERISTICS OF FINANCIAL INFORMATION

The financial information that is used to examine how a business is performing should have certain characteristics. For example, it should:

- be reliable and from a recognisable source
- give a true and fair view of the figures
- be consistent (compiled in the same way as in previous periods)
- be clear and understandable
- not contain opinions or biased views.

The main areas examined by financial information are profitability, liquidity, efficiency and capital structure.

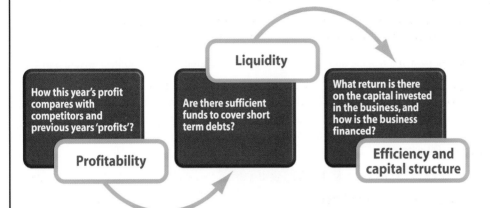

Liquidity

How this year's profit compares with competitors and previous years 'profits'?

Profitability

Are there sufficient funds to cover short term debts?

What return is there on the capital invested in the business, and how is the business financed?

Efficiency and capital structure

DON'T FORGET

Even if a business is profitable, it must still have ready cash to settle immediate bills.

LET'S THINK ABOUT THIS

Organisations need to address sustainability and environmental issues. Many are developing ways of becoming responsible for their actions in both the development and sales of their products or services. However, such policies can cause increased costs.

Using the website given on page 73, access the annual accounts for two or three different companies and compare how they are tackling environmental issues.

CASH-FLOW MANAGEMENT AND BUDGETING

Cash-flow management is probably one of the most important functions in a business. If there is not enough cash to meet commitments, then a business can go into liquidation. Organisations, whether big or small, should produce cash-flow statements. These statements will help to identify periods when the business may suffer shortages or excesses of cash.

BUDGETARY CONTROL

DON'T FORGET

It is usual for the other functional budgets to feed into the cash budget.

Budgeting is simply a method of planning for the future and for unforeseen circumstances. We all budget in our personal lives, allowing us to make decisions and control our spending. Businesses are just the same and operate a number of different budgets to help ensure that they stay efficient and financially viable.

Budgets are plans that help to ensure there is enough money to meet commitments. They control the finance and help in the decision-making process. There are a number of different types of budgets that can be used by an organisation. These are sometimes known as the **functional budgets**. For example:

DON'T FORGET

Budgets can be prepared very easily using a spreadsheet. Formulae can be used to give solutions in a variety of different circumstances, meaning that budgets can be updated very quickly. In turn, this helps to highlight months where there may be shortages or surpluses of cash. Managers can then make decisions and take action to avoid potential problems. This may mean arranging overdraft facilities, selling stock or cutting back on any major expansion plans.

The **sales budget** is probably the most difficult budget to prepare. It is not easy to estimate what, or how much, consumers will demand. If the sales budget is incorrect, then all the other budgets will be affected.

The **production budget** may not predict the correct quantity of goods to sell. Too few raw materials may be ordered. Overheads can also spiral out of control if they are not constantly monitored. Under- or overestimating the labour requirements can also affect cash flow.

WHY USE AND PREPARE BUDGETS?

Budgets provide a standard which should be worked to by each department. They:

- help to focus activity and set targets
- allow the comparison of actual and planned figures
- help managers to coordinate activities (for example, sales and production)
- highlight problem areas (for example, unnecessary waste)
- can be used to motivate individuals.

DON'T FORGET

Do not confuse a cash-flow statement (a historic document prepared under FRS 1 that measures the inflow and outflow of cash and is used externally) with a cash-flow forecast (a predictive document that is used internally).

LET'S THINK ABOUT THIS

Read this article about the Scottish budget.

Swollen public sector is where to look for cuts

When the SNP presents its third budget to parliament tomorrow no-one should expect anything other than a series of cost-cutting measures.

After months of obfuscation and denials, Gordon Brown yesterday publicly admitted what everyone with any sense already knew – public spending has to be cut to reflect these extraordinarily difficult financial times.

The Prime Minister told the TUC that cuts were inevitable if frontline services were to be protected in the face of a £350 billion budget deficit over the next four years.

Even the Government has to work to a budget. The figures are much larger, and the effects of cuts and spending have an enormous effect on the population.

Edinburgh Evening News, 16 September 2009

Think how the SNP might make the necessary cutbacks to deal with this budget deficit.

CASH BUDGET/CASH-FLOW FORECAST

The cash budget or cash-flow forecast is a prediction of how cash will be used in the business in the future. This document is different from the other financial statements because it is not historic and is only for internal use. The cash budget is usually prepared for a three- or six-month period and shows all receipts and payments, as well as all opening and closing bank balances.

This document is used to help managers to:

Plan → **Control** → **Monitor**

CASH BUDGET FOR MAY TO JULY 2010

Receipts	MAY £s	JUNE £s	JULY £s
Opening bank balance	10,000	38,000	(5,500)
+ Cash sales	28,000	29,000	28,500
+ Credit sales	120,000	135,000	132,000
TOTAL RECEIPTS	£158,000	£202,000	£155,000
Payments			
Equipment	-	80,000	-
Materials	25,000	30,000	26,500
Labour	55,000	57,500	54,000
Rent	40,000	40,000	40,000
TOTAL PAYMENTS	£120,000	£207,500	£120,500
Closing bank balance	£38,000	£(5,500)	£34,500

The closing balance is calculated by subtracting the payments from the receipts. The closing balance then becomes the opening balance for the next month. From this example, a manager would see that June has a deficit (loss) owing to the purchase of equipment. This means that suitable action could be taken to avoid a shortfall in cash; for example, an overdraft could be arranged with the bank.

WHY DO CASH PROBLEMS ARISE?

Cash problems may arise due to factors within the organisation. For example:

- wage increases
- higher utility bills (rent, heat or light)
- taking money out of the business (for example, drawings)
- overtrading.

Sometimes, cash problems can be a result of external factors. For example:

- increases in the price of fuel
- too much unsold stock due to seasonal factors
- changes in society (for example, ethical concerns).

DON'T FORGET

It is just as bad for a business to have too much cash at the end of each month as too little. Too much money in the bank means that the money is not working efficiently, and this would have to be addressed by management.

HOW CAN CASH PROBLEMS BE SOLVED?

1 If wages rise, sales prices may have to be increased.

2 To combat higher utility bills, overheads may need to be reduced.

3 Negotiating better terms with creditors or agreeing discount terms might help.

4 Reducing stock levels can free up cash (perhaps by using new stock-control methods, such as JIT).

LET'S THINK ABOUT THIS

Poor cash flow is one reason that some businesses fail. Access the following website to find other reasons for businesses failing.

www.thetimes100.co.uk/theory/theory.php?tID=320

RATIO ANALYSIS

Financial statements are only of use if interpreted correctly. This is achieved by comparing them with previous financial statements and with those of competitors. They can then be used to help make decisions.

Ratios show trends and patterns and can help to highlight problem areas. Ratio analysis can be focused on the following areas:

1. **Profitability ratios** measure the money made by the business – gross profit ratio, net profit ratio.

2. **Liquidity ratios** measure how well the business can meet its debts and commitments – current ratio, acid-test ratio.

3. **Efficiency ratios** measure how well the resources are being used – return on capital employed, profit mark-up.

Stakeholders will be interested in ratio analysis, as it allows them to see how the business is performing compared with previous years. Investors are interested in the profitability, and managers and staff in the liquidity.

RATIO FORMULAE

You will need to:

*   know how the ratio is calculated, but not actually do the calculation

*   be able to comment on what it means and shows

*   be able to comment on any limitations

*   say how it can be improved

*   describe each formula.

DON'T FORGET

Always give meaning to your formulae and comment on why an increase/decrease may have occurred.

Ratio formula	Meaning
Gross profit ratio **gross profit ÷ sales × 100%**	This ratio shows the profit made from trading (buying and selling). If the ratio increases, it means that more goods have been sold, or the price of goods sold has increased. If it decreases, it usually means that the cost of purchases has increased, or the number of goods sold has decreased.
Net profit ratio **net profit ÷ sales × 100%**	This ratio shows the amount of profit made after expenses. If the ratio increases, then the business is being more efficient in controlling its expenses. If it decreases, then the costs must be investigated to find out what has increased and why.
Current ratio **current assets : current liabilities**	This ratio shows how well the business will be able to pay off its debts. Ideally, the ratio should be 2:1, which means that there are twice as many assets as liabilities. A lower ratio means there is a problem with liquidity.

contd

RATIO FORMULAE contd

Acid-test ratio **current assets – stock : current liabilities**	This is a stronger test of liquidity than the current ratio, as it does not include stock. This is because stock is the most difficult current asset to turn into ready cash. A ratio of about 1:1 would mean that the business is able to meet its short-term debts; a ratio less than 1 would mean that the cash situation should be carefully monitored.
Return on capital employed (ROCE) **net profit ÷ capital employed × 100%**	This ratio calculates the amount that the owner gets back on the capital invested in the business. This should be a better rate than any opportunity offered by other businesses or investment schemes. The higher the better.
Profit mark-up **gross profit ÷ cost of goods sold × 100%**	This ratio measures the percentage added to trading costs as profit and can be used to find the selling price. Should this ratio increase, there has been either an increase in the selling price per unit or a fall in the cost price per unit. A decrease will mean the opposite.

SOME DRAWBACKS TO RATIO ANALYSIS

1   There must be at least two sets of figures in order to make a comparison.

2   Realistic comparisons can only be made between present/past years and with other similar businesses.

3   Results will be historic.

4   If different formulae are used, figures can become distorted.

5   Findings do not always take important external factors into account (for example, the credit crunch).

6   There is no recognition of internal factors (for example, staff motivation and morale).

DON'T FORGET

You will not be expected to use figures to calculate ratios in the Higher exam, but you do need to know how these formulae are constructed.

 Look up these sites. www.bbc.co.uk/schools/gcsebitesize/business/finance/ www.thetimes100.co.uk/studies/view-summary--financial-information-decision-making--114--281.php

LET'S THINK ABOUT THIS

Read this article extract. Can you think of other companies whose share prices might have been affected by swine flu? Give reasons for your answers.

Further gloom on jobs and toxic debts

Thomas Cook will give an update on how the travel sector is faring when it reports interim figures on the 13th May. [These come] after the recent swine flu outbreak.

The group's shares were hit when the outbreak first surfaced, as were stocks across the travel and airline sector. But shares have since recovered some of the ground lost as concerns have eased over the severity of the outbreak.

Scotsman, 11 May 2009

HUMAN-RESOURCE MANAGEMENT

THE ROLE OF HUMAN RESOURCES

Human-resource management used to be referred to as 'personnel', but this term does not accurately describe the activities such departments now perform. The role of HR has been influenced by a number of factors (for example, changes in technology and the law and the changing goals of business). It is now recognised that an organisation's most important resource is its staff. The remit of the HR department involves ensuring compliance with employment legislation and overseeing training and staff development. It also includes:

Recruitment and selection of staff

- Investigating trends in the current labour market.
- Forecasting future staffing needs and identifying future skills required.
- Providing induction training.

Promoting a corporate culture

- Sharing the mission and vision.
- Facilitating communication systems.
- Providing CPD (continuing professional development).

Managing staff welfare

- Team-building.
- Providing fringe benefits.
- Work–life balance and health schemes.

Managing employee relations

- Designing, implementing and managing appraisals.
- Dealing with discipline and grievances
- Managing redundancy.

The HR department is involved at the very highest level of decision-making (strategic). It is one of the main functional areas of the organisation, and its size will depend on the number of employees. HR is responsible for the implementation and development of many staffing policies, as well as making sure that these policies are accessible and up to date. HR is also responsible for getting the best out of staff by maintaining motivation and morale.

DON'T FORGET

HR can have a direct effect on the quality of goods produced or services provided. If the department does its job correctly, it will recruit and develop a highly competent workforce.

DON'T FORGET

Staff are motivated by a variety of different factors (for example, pay, holidays, status, working conditions and other fringe benefits, like staff discount).

THE CHANGING WORKING ENVIRONMENT

In the last 20 years, the make-up of the workforce has changed in a number of different ways.

Working practices	There has been a decline in full-time jobs, an increase in part-time and temporary posts and an increase in the number of people working from home (teleworking).
Types of employment	There are more jobs now in the service and tertiary sectors than 20 years ago.
Workers	More women and migrant workers (particularly from Eastern Europe) have entered the labour market.
Industry	There are many more smaller, specialised firms and self-employed people than 20 years ago. Many larger organisations have downsized by outsourcing work abroad, where labour is cheaper.
Work–life balance	Many workers' lifestyle choices mean more career changes and less loyalty to organisations.
Ageing population	As people live longer, the working population gains more dependants. This puts a strain on services such as the NHS and pensions.

DON'T FORGET

As working practices and technology develop, more money needs to be spent on training and retraining.

DON'T FORGET

You will need to know what **PEST** factors have affected the working environment. Remember that PEST stands for political, economic, social and technological. You should be able to describe the effect of these factors (for example, economic: as firms downsize, more work is outsourced).

LET'S THINK ABOUT THIS

A good way to remember the role of HR is to think about **FACES**. Do some research to find out how HR fulfils each of these roles.

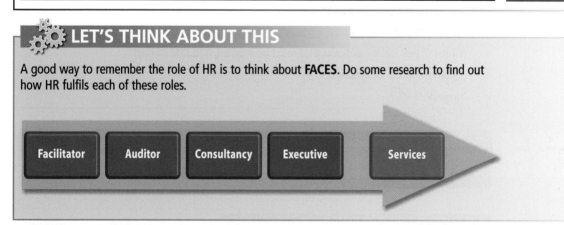

Facilitator   Auditor   Consultancy   Executive   Services

RECRUITMENT OF STAFF

When a vacancy for a job arises, it is the responsibility of the HR department to make sure that the best person fills the post. Before this can be done, HR will need to ensure that the post is still required.

JOB ANALYSIS AND DESIGN

It is important to look at what the current job entails. Over time, the duties of a particular post can become redundant. The organisation may require the next post-holder to perform different duties and have an alternative set of skills. This gives the organisation the opportunity to advertise for the right person. Before doing this, it is necessary to prepare a person specification, detailing the qualifications, skills (both essential and desirable) and qualities required.

A **job description** can then be prepared. This should include:

- a job title
- the main purpose of the job
- the main duties to be performed
- the line manager
- the location of the job
- details of pay (salary or hours that must be worked, and rate of pay)
- conditions (such as holidays)
- fringe benefits.

 Look up www.dius.gov.uk/higher_education/widening_participation/
professional_recruitment_guide/recruitment_step_by_step/defining_the_job/
person_specification#example

ADVERTISING THE POST

First, it is necessary to decide whether to advertise the job within the organisation (**internally**) or outside (**externally**). Second, it must be decided **how** to advertise the job. The cost of advertising can be an influencing factor.

Internal recruitment

Strengths	Weaknesses
The candidate is already known to the organisation.	Internal promotion creates another vacancy.
Advertising costs can be avoided.	There may not be a suitable internal candidate.
There is no need for induction to the organisation.	New skills and a fresh approach will not always be gained.
Time can be saved, as the candidate starts the new role immediately.	
Has a positive effect on staff morale.	

contd

ADVERTISING THE POST contd

External recruitment

Strengths	Weaknesses
Greater pool of available labour to choose from.	More costly and time-consuming, as adverts need to be placed.
Can appoint the best person for the job.	Interviews need to be set up.
Can increase skills and specialisms.	External candidates need to give a period of notice before commencing employment.
Avoid conflict among internal candidates.	

DON'T FORGET

There are a variety of different ways to attract and recruit staff from outside the organisation (newspaper adverts, internet adverts, specialist magazines, recruitment agencies and schools, colleges or universities).

REWARDS AND REMUNERATION

The main purpose of employment for most employees is remuneration. It is the responsibility of the HR department to work out the best and most cost-effective method of paying employees.

The most common form of payment is a salary, which is usually paid to non-manual workers on a monthly basis. However, manual workers also receive a wage, and this can be calculated in a number of ways. See page 61 for different payment options.

LET'S THINK ABOUT THIS

Read this article extract and note how remuneration methods are used to motivate staff.

Ballot call on Qinetiq pay freeze

Staff at defence research firm Qinetiq are to be balloted on strike action in protest at a pay freeze.

Unions said their members would be asked to vote over the next few weeks amid claims that executives are to receive bonus payments. The group employs more than 7,000 staff in the UK, with sites in Hampshire, Worcestershire, Wiltshire, Portsmouth, Devon, Glasgow and Dorset.

David Luxton, national officer of the Prospect union, said: 'Qinetiq's justification for the pay freeze does not hold up to close scrutiny.

'It continues to be a highly profitable company both internationally and in the UK with a backlog of secured work worth £5.4bn.'

Qinetiq said it would be awarding pay increases for the current year to all UK employees who have been assessed as 'outstanding' or 'exemplary' under the company's performance management system, while a profit-sharing scheme covering all employees was being introduced.

BBC News, 18 May 2009

4 BUSINESS DECISION AREAS: FINANCE AND HUMAN RESOURCES

SELECTION AND INDUCTION OF STAFF

Individuals who are interested in promotion, or in advertised posts, will need to complete an application form. In some instances, they will also provide a CV. This document is prepared by the applicant and gives personal details, qualifications, training, experience and sometimes a photograph. These forms are matched to the person specification; and those applicants who meet the criteria will be invited to attend for interview.

SELECTION METHODS AND TECHNIQUES

Before applicants are invited to an interview, they may have to undergo a series of tests.

Attainment tests are used to assess the ability of the applicant to work under pressure. For example, a mechanic may be asked to change a tyre.

Aptitude tests are given to assess if the applicant is suited to the particular organisation or style of work.

Intelligence (IQ) tests are used to assess the applicant's mental ability to cope with situations involving literacy, numeracy and problem-solving.

Fitness tests are used when the job requires the applicant to be physically fit; for example, in the fire service or the police force.

Medical tests may be required by organisations where the applicant is going to be working with a number of people; for example, teachers, nurses or footballers (who often change club).

Psychometric tests are given to measure an applicant's personality and to give an indication of how they may react or behave in certain circumstances.

DON'T FORGET

You should be able to **describe** the recruitment process in detail and **discuss** different forms of testing and interview.

The purpose of these tests is to provide information to help in the selection of candidates for interview or employment. Once the tests are complete, the applicant will usually attend an interview. Interviews can be conducted on a one-to-one basis or by a panel (which tends to include the line manager and a representative from HR). There may be more than one interview. Eventually, the most suitable candidate is selected and offered the job. Unsuccessful candidates are usually informed once the successful candidate has accepted the position.

For further details on recruitment, selection and training of staff, look up www.thetimes100.co.uk/theory/theory--recruitment-selection--349.php

INDUCTION TRAINING

Induction is the term used to describe the process of introducing new employees to an organisation. In some companies, it will last for only a day; in others, it could be spread over the course of several weeks.

The induction programme

The induction programme is designed to ensure that new employees are integrated into the organisation as quickly and efficiently as possible, and consists of:

General topics

- an introduction to the organisation – its mission, vision and goals
- the structure of the organisation and the employee's role

contd

INDUCTION TRAINING contd

- meeting and greeting colleagues
- health and safety and housekeeping (for example, where the canteen and the toilets are located)
- fire evacuation procedures
- staff welfare.

Specific topics

- job description and role
- location of workspace
- reporting procedures.

Benefits of induction training

A good induction allows staff members to settle into their jobs and become aware of the corporate culture. In turn, this increases motivation and morale, promotes a good image of the organisation and means that the new worker becomes productive much more quickly.

DON'T FORGET

Be prepared to discuss how induction training differs from training provided for existing staff.

Take a look at more detailed information on induction programmes, and examine the effects on staff if induction is not done properly:
www.cipd.co.uk/subjects/recruitmen/induction/induction.htm

LET'S THINK ABOUT THIS

Have you ever wondered how to prepare for an interview? There are some questions that are always asked; for example, 'What qualities can you bring to this post?' Visit this website to get a real taste of what an interview can be like:

www.jobsite.co.uk/bemyinterviewer

TRAINING AND STAFF DEVELOPMENT

DON'T FORGET

The concept of **lifelong learning** recognises that we never stop needing to improve in order to remain competitive and efficient.

Training is the process of teaching new skills to employees to allow them to improve in their jobs. Continuous (ongoing) training is the development of those skills that enhance and improve the employee's performance.

 Go to this website to read a paper on how continuous training and development can improve our mental wellbeing and help us perform better in our working lives: **www.lifelonglearning.co.uk/ln08112.htm**

TYPES OF TRAINING

On-the-job training (in-house training) can be tailored to specific requirements. However, employees may find it difficult to 'switch off' from their jobs. This type of training includes:

- job swaps or rotations – the individual changes job to learn new skills
- demonstrations – the individual observes how a job is performed
- secondments – the individual works on a specific task.

Off-the-job training takes place off-site. It allows the employee to meet new people and to exchange ideas with workers from other companies. However, it can prove costly. This type of training includes:

- attending college – on day release or on an open-learning basis
- attending special courses – organised by the business or others to give the employee certificated recognition of skills.

COSTS OF TRAINING

In addition to the financial costs of arranging training, other costs include:

- expenses incurred by employees for travel and meals
- lost time and output while the employee is on the training course
- staff who resist the training offered
- staff who leave after receiving training.

STAFF APPRAISAL

Staff appraisal is the process whereby an employee meets with his/her line manager to discuss training and development needs. Some organisations call these meetings annual reviews or performance development reviews (if they are being linked to pay).

The process requires both parties to prepare for the meeting and to discuss how the employee has performed throughout the year. If the meeting is to remain positive, the manager needs to listen carefully and set agreed targets or goals for the employee for the coming year. Ideally, further review dates should be scheduled during the year to assess an employee's progress. It is important to keep a formal record of the meeting for future reference. Employees should also keep a log of staff development activities undertaken throughout the year.

DON'T FORGET

If you are asked to **discuss** appraisals, make sure you mention both positive and negative aspects.

THE VALUE AND BENEFITS OF AN APPRAISAL SYSTEM

An appraisal should be seen as a positive tool which can motivate employees. It should:

- allow for feedback
- let managers discuss their expectations
- let the employee discuss personal development needs
- help improve communication
- help control and monitor performance
- help with updating job descriptions
- be used when reviewing salaries.

Appraisals can be unsuccessful if the manager:

- fails to address issues
- avoids confrontation
- does not keep a formal record of the discussion.

"BEFORE WE START MY JOB APPRAISAL....ID LIKE TO SHOW YOU A COUPLE OF PHOTOS I TOOK OF YOU AND YOUR SECRETARY AT THE OFFICE PICNIC."

DISCIPLINE AND GRIEVANCE PROCEDURES

Employees may take out a grievance against their employer. In this instance, the HR department will have set procedures to follow. A serious matter could end up at a tribunal, and an employer may even be forced to pay compensation.

However, disciplinary action is usually taken by the employer against the employee. A serious action can result in instant dismissal. The usual disciplinary procedure entails a verbal warning, a first written warning and a final warning, before dismissal.

LET'S THINK ABOUT THIS

Should performance-related pay be introduced for teachers? What do you think the arguments for and against may be? Look up www.thestudentroom.co.uk/showthread.php?t=720034

EMPLOYEE RELATIONS

Good employee relations help organisations to run smoothly and meet objectives. Employers have a duty to **consult** with employees and take part in fair **negotiation** before any changes are made, but they are under no obligation to listen to employee demands.

On occasion, disagreements and disputes will arise. In order to represent both sides fairly, there are support groups available for employees (trade unions) and for employers (employer associations). When no agreement can be reached, ACAS (the Advisory, Conciliation and Arbitration Service) may be approached.

TRADE UNIONS

Trade unions represent employees when negotiating working conditions and rates of pay; and there are different trade unions to represent different groups of workers. For example, the EIS (Educational Institute of Scotland) mainly represents teachers, while Unite is the new general union created in 2007 from the merger of the TGWU and Amicus. Other well-known unions are the NUJ (National Union of Journalists) and the TUC (Trades Union Congress), which represents all UK trade unions.

Trade unions represent workers when negotiating with management. Because they represent a large group of people, they are able to push for higher wages or better concessions than if a worker were to negotiate on an individual basis. This is called **collective bargaining**. Unions are able to reach decisions nationally or locally, depending on the situation.

EMPLOYER ASSOCIATIONS

Employer associations are set up to look after the interests of all businesses in a particular type of industry. They will represent the employer when negotiations are taking place, and can act together to put pressure on the government. The CBI (Confederation of British Industry) is a body set up to represent employers from all sectors of UK industry and commerce.

Another way to promote positive employee relations is to set up **works councils**. These groups are made up of equal numbers of management and workers, and their function is to discuss any changes before they are implemented. Sometimes, **worker directors** are also elected to sit on the board of management and may contribute to the decision-making process.

 Look up www.tuc.org.uk and www.cbi.org.uk

ACAS

DON'T FORGET

ACAS can also be involved in cases of unfair dismissal, discrimination and redundancy.

The Advisory, Conciliation and Arbitration Service was set up in 1975 to help improve employment relations. It can:

advise	ACAS gives advice on all work-related matters (for example, how to design and implement policies and interpret legislation).
conciliate	ACAS acts as an independent third party and a channel of communication between the union and the employer.
mediate	ACAS tries to put forward a basis for settlement, though it does not have to be accepted by either party.
arbitrate	ACAS listens to both parties, gathers all the facts and figures, makes a decision and offers a solution which both sides will have agreed to accept.

 Look up www.acas.org.uk

INDUSTRIAL ACTION

When employers and employees have a dispute and fail to agree a solution, employees can take industrial action. Industrial action which has been voted for and backed by a trade union is known as an **official dispute**. If workers walk out without going through the proper procedures, this is known as an **unofficial dispute**. Workers can take action in various ways:

strike	Workers withdraw their labour.
work-to-rule	Workers only do the tasks stated in their job description.
sit-in	Workers stay in their place of work but don't do any work.
go-slow	Workers work more slowly than normal – usually applies more to manual workers.
overtime bans	Workers do not do any work outside their normal hours.
picketing	Workers stand outside their place of work and try to stop others from entering.

> **DON'T FORGET**
>
> In some workplaces, there are single-union agreements. This is when one union involves all the workers at that workplace and negotiates on their behalf. This can save time and money.

EFFECTS OF INDUSTRIAL ACTION

Production falls → Loss in sales → Fall in customers → Staff leave → Reputation and image suffers → Production falls

> **DON'T FORGET**
>
> Employers can also take action against a workforce. They can lock them out, reduce working hours or even close the premises. The final stage is redundancy.

LET'S THINK ABOUT THIS

Read the following article. Can you find out which workers are represented by the union GMB?

Strike-hit oil firm pulls out of ACAS talks

Unions last night launched a blistering attack on the management of an oil refinery for failing to hold discussions after dismissing hundreds of staff.

Total, which runs the Lindsey oil refinery in North Lincolnshire, pulled out of talks yesterday with ACAS, the conciliation service, and the GMB and Unite unions.

The French energy giant's decision to sack 647 contract workers who have been taking unofficial industrial action for the past week sparked a series of wildcat strikes across England and Wales yesterday.

As the standoff grew increasingly bitter, the general secretary of the GMB union accused Total of a lack of integrity, and warned that 'bullying and intimidation' would not lead to resolution.

The workers at the plant have been sent letters informing them that they have until Monday afternoon to reapply for their jobs.

Scotsman, 19 June 2009

LEGISLATION

DON'T FORGET

As legislation can be varied and difficult to understand, you need to be able to **describe** the main purpose and features of each act. You will also need to be able to **explain** how the act may impact on an organisation.

The HR department is expected to make sure that all policies and procedures in the organisation comply with three main areas of legislation:

- health and safety
- employment
- equal opportunities.

Look up www.hse.gov.uk
www.direct.gov.uk
www.equalityhumanrights.com

Act	Purpose	Features	Impact on organisation
Health and Safety at Work Act 1974	To maintain standards of health and safety for both individuals in employment and the general public.	Both employers and employees have a duty to work towards a healthy and safe environment.	Employers must appoint safety officers and provide special clothing and a safe working environment. Employees must behave in a safe manner and take responsibility for their actions. They must also attend all training courses in health and safety.
Employment Rights Act 1996	Deals with the rights most employees are entitled to at work.	Contract of employment; unfair dismissal; redundancy; reasonable notice; flexible working; training.	The contract gives the employee rights which can be challenged in court if the contract is breached by the employer.
Employment Relations Act 1999	To ensure that the UK's system of employment law is based on fairness, flexibility and partnership.	Provides compensation for unfair dismissal; maternity and paternity leave; rights for part-time workers.	Employers must comply with the provisions of the Act.
National Minimum Wage Regulations 1999	To ensure that employers pay workers at least the national minimum wage and to help workers establish that they are getting what they are entitled to.	To identify who is entitled to the minimum wage (applies to everyone except self-employed workers, apprentices under the age of 19 and students on work placement).	Employers are required by law to ensure that their workers are paid at least the current minimum wage; and they need to keep sufficient records to prove this.
Working Time Regulations 1998	To ensure that employers fulfil their obligations with regard to the working time of their employees.	To make sure that employees over the minimum school-leaving age work the correct number of hours per week and are given entitlement to rest breaks and annual leave.	The act applies to all workers, and any employer not complying can be prosecuted.

Act	Purpose	Features	Impact on organisation
Data Protection Act 1998	To control how information is handled, particularly personal data stored on computers.	There are eight key principles of the Data Protection Act. See page 33 for more information.	The organisation needs to register with the Information Commissioner and identify data controllers who will manage the storage of information on data subjects.
Computer Misuse Act 1990	To ensure prosecution of those who use computers for illegal purposes.	It is an offence to access a computer without permission, to access a computer with intent to commit a criminal act or to alter data without permission.	Employers must make sure that stored data is secure and that it complies with the Copyright, Design and Patents Act. They must also take regular back-ups and install anti-virus software.
Freedom of Information (Scotland) Act 2002, or Freedom of Information Act 2000	Provides significant and important rights of access to public information.	Anyone can make a request for information, from anywhere in the world. A reason does not need to be given.	Individuals must be told within 20 days if the public authority holds the requested information. Some information may be sensitive and not show the organisation in a positive light.
Equal Pay Act 1970	To prohibit less favourable treatment between men and women in terms of pay and conditions.	To claim under this act, an employee must prove one of the following: work done is the same; work done is of an equal value; work done is rated the same.	Employers need to make sure that there are clear job descriptions for all positions.
Equal Opportunities	There are various acts.	To prevent discrimination on grounds of sex, race, disability, age, gender or religion.	Employers must make sure that their policies and procedures comply with all equal-opportunities legislation.

⚙ LET'S THINK ABOUT THIS

Read this article. If journalists didn't have access to the Freedom of Information Act, the scandal over MPs' expenses might never have been made public!

Spotlight to fall on MPs' expenses in Freedom of Information ruling

Details of MPs' expenses are to be made public after a Freedom of Information ruling.

Information Commissioner Richard Thomas has ruled that the annual Additional Costs Allowance should be broken down into 12 categories. The House of Commons now has 35 days to comply with the ruling and publish MPs' figures for the past year.

The 12 categories are: mortgage costs, hotel bills, food, service charges, utilities, telecoms, furnishings, maintenance, cleaning, insurance, basic security and 'other'.

The allowance is paid to all MPs who live outside London, and MPs can claim up to £21,634 each year.

The House of Commons Commission is expected to appeal against the ruling on the grounds that they have an expectation to privacy.

Daily Mail, 15 June 2009

INDEX